The Almighty, His Creation of Mankind, and His War against the Eloheem

Loinell Mills Hinds

Copyright © 2019 by Loinell Mills Hinds.

ISBN   Softcover   978-1-950580-81-1

All rights reserved. No part of this book may be reproduced or transmitted in any form or by any means, electronic or mechanical, including photocopying, recording, or by any information storage and retrieval system without express written permission from the author, except in the case of brief quotations embodied in critical reviews and certain other non-commercial uses permitted by copyright law.

Printed in the United States of America.

To order additional copies of this book, contact:
Bookwhip
1-855-339-3589
https://www.bookwhip.com

As a book of legal law, this doctrine is legal, and is record of the Righteousness that comes from the ALMIGHTY, the ALL SUPREME BEING, the ALL SUPREME RULER, the CREATOR of all things known and unknown. This doctrine is a legal document like in the manner of a certificate of divorce or a deed of purchase. This is the only doctrine of instruction for the genealogy, history, and prophecies concerning mankind that the All Supreme Being commanded to be written and maintained as a record of truth about the origin of the Earth, its Heavens, its inhabitants, their knowledge, and their generations. At the end of their generations, this doctrine is a record, and, will be used as evidence when the Almighty, the All Supreme Being, the All Supreme Ruler takes His Stand for His Judgment according to His Cause. As follows, only on these conditions, for the Almighty's Cause, this doctrine will serve as a legal indictment and a formal accusation. It will be used to illustrate and show that a system, a situation or individual man is bad and deserves to be condemned. At the request of learned kings, rulers, and judges able to read and understand the scriptural writing in its written order, this doctrine can be used to execute its written instruction that comes from the Almighty Himself. This doctrine can be observed and is reserved for learning the righteousness that comes from the Almighty. This doctrine began with the first true man at the command of the Almighty and is appointed to his chosen posterity. All those ordained and appointed to keep and declare this record are to observe, care for, execute, and maintain this record according to its original truth for an everlasting duty through all their generations. In the beginning, before there were former things, there was the

Almighty, the All Supreme Being, who is the first existing entity before the existence of time and space. He alone is self-existent. He alone is the Most Ancient Being because He is the first existing entity before time. He is the first before all creation. He alone is the most blessed being and the most glorious being. HE alone is the most holy being and the most righteous being. HE alone is all powerful and all knowing, He is the ALMIGHTY. He alone is of everlasting life and ever flowing energy. He alone, is the source of everlasting life and, everlasting power. His Word alone is life or death. His Word is the most holy. All life belongs to the Almighty, the All Supreme Being, the Creator of all things. He alone created all things known and unknown. Without the Almighty nothing can exit, nothing can have life. He is the first King of all kings and He is the finest of all kings. In the beginning, before time, before former things, surrounded by complete darkness, the Almighty chose to create new conditions and circumstances using transformations. With HIS divine mind of activity, the Almighty, the Creator of all things gave birth to an idea to create a world with life. The Almighty considered this world with life, and He considered what was needed to sustain its life. In His divine Mind, first He saw it, then, He decided to created two visible heavens for this world with life, one heaven with an atmosphere of air and a higher heaven with its own atmosphere. The higher heaven would be visible through the atmosphere with air. Opposite to this world that sustains life, the Almighty considered, then HE saw and desired to create a place where there is no living. He decided to create a place for the dead. Before time, before the All Supreme Being commanded with His Voice, before the Earth and its two heavens came to exist, nothing had form. It was complete nothingness. It was only empty space. It was chaos and confusion. Misery, destruction, death, sorrow, and ignorance are the treasures of darkness that were hidden in the obscurity of this deep darkness that surrounded everything. Therefore, before time, deep darkness was in the presence of the deep places, deep darkness surrounded massive violent surging water. Everything was in immeasurable darkness.

The living SPIRT of the Almighty, the All Supreme Being, the Creator of all things is in the image of the wind. Like breath hitting the cold air, it is animated, both of unknown and unmeasured energy, both of unknown and unmeasured activity. His SPIRIT is the source of life and glory. It is the source of passions, emotions and appetites. His SPIRIT is the source of anger, courage, patience, and, impatience. It the source of will and impulse. His SPIRITis the source of mental abilities and spiritual faculties. Now, the living SPIRIT of the Almighty traveled throughout all the deep darkness from above to below. When His SPIRIT moved to be above the surface of the violent waters, and HE came to a hover over the surface of violent waters. Then, the Almighty relaxed and considered the deep darkness, the misery, the chaos, and the confusion that was all around Him. HE desired to speak against the deep darkness that was all around Him. HE desired to create against the deep darkness that was all around Him. Therefore, with affection and a feeling of tender love, the ALMIGHTY spoke and commanded with His voice saying, let there be a clear and bright light for instruction. Let it come into existence, let it become established, and let it remain established in existence. He spoke again and commanded with His voice saying, let there be a clear and bright light for life. Let it come into existence, let it become established, and let it remain established in existence. The Almighty, the All Supreme Being, the Creator spoke again and commanded with His voice saying, let there be a clear and bright light for prosperity. Let it come into existence, let it become established, and let it remain established in existence. He spoke again and commanded with His voice saying, let there be a clear and bright light for happiness. Let it come into existence, let it become established, and let it remain established in existence. At the sound of His voice, the light for instruction, the light for life, the light for prosperity, and the light for happiness came into existence became established, and remained established. The Almighty looked at the light for instruction to discern it and distinguish it. He gazed upon it and considered to find out if He could respect it, to find out if He could enjoy it, and, to find out if He could approve of it. The Almighty looked at the light for life to discern it and distinguish it. He gazed upon it and considered, to find out if He could respect it, to find out if He could enjoy it, and to find out if He could approve of it. Then, He looked at the light for prosperity to discern and distinguish it. He gazed upon it and considered to find out if He could respect it, to find out if He could enjoy it, and to find out if He could approve of it. Afterwards, He looked at the light for happiness to discern it and distinguish it. He gazed upon it and considered to find out if He could respect it, to find out if He could enjoy it, and to find out if He could approve of it. As He observed the light for instruction, the light for life, the light for prosperity, and the light for happiness. He saw how these lights shined brilliantly and gloriously among the deep darkness of misery, chaos, ignorance, sorrow, and nothingness. In the sight of the Almighty, these lights overcame, overwhelmed, and overthrew the deep darkness of misery, chaos, ignorance, sorrow, and nothingness. The deep darkness misery, chaos, ignorance, sorrow, and nothingness could not overcome the performance that came from these lights. The Almighty observed all these things and decided that these lights produced very appropriate morals and very pleasant ethics. In His sight, these lights were altogether beautiful.

Then, the Almighty put a difference between the deep darkness of misery, chaos, ignorance, sorrow, nothingness, and the light for instruction, light for life, light for prosperity, and light for happiness. HE withdrew those lights from out of the deep darkness of obscurity, from out of the darkness of misery, from out of the darkness of ignorance, from out of the darkness of destruction, from out of the darkness of death, and from out of the darkness of sorrow. Then, the Almighty set apart HIS own light for instruction, light for life, light for happiness, and light for prosperity. Then, He divided them to be periods of time. The Almighty, the All Supreme Being, the Creator of all things called out and named the light for instruction, the light for life, the light for prosperity, and the light for happiness. He called these lights good enlightenment. HE called out and named the obscurity, the misery, the sorrow, the destruction, the ignorance, and the nothingness. HE called these things the darkness of evil. In the beginning, before time, this is the first miracle and the first divine work that came from the Almighty, the All Supreme Being, the Creator of all things. Then the Creator created His own Heaven. Afterwards, for His own Heaven, the Almighty created Cherubs (**Keh-roov**). For His own Heaven, the Almighty created other spiritual beings to make up His Holy Assembly. HE caused all of them to be learned. He caused all of them to be obedient only to Himself. Then the Almighty spoke a command saying, let there be a flat strong surface of support, let it be a covering that goes over the Earth to the ends of the Earth. Let it be unbroken. Let it appear in the middle, in the midst of this violent surge of waters. Then, let it separate these violent waters. Let it make a difference between these waters. Therefore, let the waters above the covering be distinguished from the waters underneath the covering. Then, a strong unbroken surface of support separated the flood of violent waters according to the commandment that came from the Almighty. Then, the Almighty, the Creator of all things summoned His Holy Assembly to preach to them. Before all them, He named the strong unbroken surface that separated the waters a Sky. Below the sky there is an atmosphere of air. This is the first heaven of the Earth. Above the sky, there is the Earth's visible universe. It is the second heaven of the Earth. In the beginning, this is the second miracle and the second work the Creator completed. Then, the Almighty, the All Supreme Being, the Creator of all things commanded with His voice saying, let the flood of waters underneath sky gather itself together. Let this flood of water stand in one place and wait upon the command from My voice. Then, let dry soil appear on it, and, this will be the surface of the ground. Dry soil appeared, and the ALMIGHTY gazed upon it. HE inspected it and enjoyed it. Made of soil, the ground formed a massive land and remained as it was. This was according to the command that came from the voice of the Almighty, the All Supreme Being, the Creator of all things. Then, the Almighty summoned His Holy Assembly to proclaim to them. Before them, the Almighty named the violent flood of water that had gathered together underneath the Sky. HE named it the Seas. Then the Almighty named the ground made of soil Earth. The Almighty, the All Supreme Being considered and looked upon the Earth and the Seas to discern them, to learn about them, to distinguish them, to see if He could respect them, to see if He could enjoy looking at them, and to see if He could approve of them. The Almighty, the Creator of all things saw that this was beautiful and knew it would be prosperous. It was pleasant and agreeable to Him. HE saw it as a good thing that could become better.

Then, the Almighty considered and commanded with His voice saying, let the soil of the ground bring forth vegetation. Let the soil of the ground sprout green grass, green plants, and tender herbs after its own species. Let the green plants and tender herbs conceive to produce seed that can be scattered and sowed. Let the soil of the ground bring forth fruit each after its own species. Let the soil of the ground bring forth trees with branches each after its own species. Let the soil bring forth stalks of woody flax each after its own species. Let the soil bring forth fruit trees whose seed is in itself each after its own species. These things came into existence and remained, therefore, it was so according to the commandment that came from the Almighty, the All Supreme Being, the Creator of all things. The Almighty gazed upon these things and inspected them. He learned about them. He discerned and distinguished each one of them, to see if He would approve of them. He saw that these things were beautiful and He knew they would be prosperous. These things were pleasant and agreeable to Him. This completed the third miracle and the third work that came from the Almighty, the All Supreme Being, the Creator of all things. Then, the Almighty fashioned and produced two great and bright luminous bodies of light. The larger and greater light is of a fiery burning heat. The heat from this light is to warm the Earth. It will rule the time-period of Day. The lesser and smaller light will rule for the time-period opposite to the Day. It will rule the time-period of gloom, that is the time-period of night. Then the Almighty created the atmosphere where celestial bodies of element revolve. He made the stars and fashioned them to shine as a chandelier. The stars were made to blaze with heat and shine with light. The Almighty put all these lights in their order and assigned them to be visible in the atmosphere above the sky. He assigned them to be visible among the celestial bodies that revolve in the universe. These lights and celestial bodies of element were placed in the Earth's highest heaven. Then the Almighty considered and looked at them. He discerned. He distinguished them. The Almighty saw that this was beautiful and He knew they would be prosperous. He saw that it was pleasant and agreeable to Him. He saw it as a good thing. Therefore, the sun, the moon, and the stars will shine light upon the Earth. After considering these lights, the Almighty commanded with His voice saying, let these lights in the atmosphere above the sky divide the daytime from the nighttime. Let them be evidence of My miracles. Let them be remembered as proof of My miracles. Let them be used to measure time, to measure days, to measure years of life, and for a signal of the seasons. This completed the fourth miracle, the fourth work that came from the Almighty, the All Supreme Being, the Creator of all things. Then, the Almighty commanded with His voice saying, let moving and creeping creatures, small insects, and small animals, of body, of mind, of heart, of emotion, and of appetite come to life in the Seas. Let them breed abundantly to increase abundantly. Let flying creatures, flying insects, and flying birds covered with feathers, of body, of mind, of heart, of emotion, and of appetite come to life, and let them fly about to and from. Let them hover and let them fly above the soil of the ground and in the open sky in the atmosphere of air. The Almighty created great dinosaurs, great whales, great serpents, dragons, and sea monsters of the sea. These were creatures with an activity of mind. These living creatures were of body, blood, and heart. Their desire, appetite, passions, and emotions are things of their soul, therefore, their soul is the life in their blood.

Then, the Almighty created every living creature that creeps and crawls, that moves about, that walks on all fours, and that glides swiftly. These animals were with an activity of mind. These living animals were of body, blood, and heart. Their desire, appetite, passions, and emotions are things of their soul, therefore, their soul is the life in their blood. They bred abundantly in the seas and increased abundantly. Every flying creature, flying insect, and flying bird covered with feathers bred abundantly and increased abundantly according to their own species. Then the Almighty looked at them and considered. To learn about them, He observed them and discerned. He watched them to see if He could respect them, to see if He would enjoy looking at them, and to see if He would approve of them. Then, He distinguished them. The Almighty saw that this was beautiful and He knew it would be prosperous. It was agreeable to Him because He saw it as a good thing. After the Almighty considered them, He blessed them by His commandment saying, be fruitful, increase and grow, bring forth fruit, branch off and show fruitfulness. Over the process of time, multiply and become many, become numerous, and do much in respect to your authority. Accomplish in the waters of the seas. Satisfy yourselves in waters of the seas. Replenish yourselves in the waters of the seas. Your end will be the waters in the seas. Let the flying creatures, the flying insects, the flying birds covered with feathers multiply and become many, become numerous, and do much in respect to their authority. Let them thoroughly nourish and enlarge themselves upon the soil of the ground throughout the whole earth. This is the fifth miracle, the fifth completed work that came from the Almighty, the All Supreme Being, the Creator of all things. Then the Almighty considered. Afterwards, He commanded with His voice saying, I will create cattle and dumb wild beasts of the land. These living animals will have a mind of activity. They will have a body of flesh. Their body will have a heart, and be of blood. They will have desire, appetite, passion, and emotions. These are things of their soul, therefore, their soul is the life in their blood. Now, let them come to life and of the dumb beast, I will bring forth the Behemoth. Behemoth are the first humans of mind, body, blood, and heart. Their desire, appetite, passions, and emotions are things of their soul, therefore, their soul is the life in their blood. The Behemoth are human species from animal transformation. As the Almighty commanded, they did come forth to life. The Almighty created both male and female. The Almighty blessed them by His commandment saying, be fruitful, increase and grow, bring forth fruit, branch off and show fruitfulness. Conquer and subdue the Earth. Over the process of time, multiply and become many, become numerous, and do much in respect to your authority. Now, the Almighty had created moving and creeping organisms of the land and of the sea; creeping reptiles of the land and of the sea, each after its own species. Then, the Almighty looked at them and considered. He observed them to learn about them. As He observed them, the Almighty discerned to see if He could respect them, to see if He would enjoy looking at them, and to see if He would approve of them. It was agreeable to Him because He saw some good things, but the Almighty saw it could be better. Therefore, as designated by the authority of the Almighty, the All Supreme Being, the All Supreme Ruler, for an individual monument and memorial, the name of the first flood that increased and dispersed from the seas is Pison (**Pee-shown**). The Almighty caused this flood of water to go around the whole Earth and surround it. Like a skirt, it surrounded all the people of the nations that inhabited the Earth.

Then it came back, returning in reverse, assembling back, uniting to its designated foundation, that is, encircling the land of the living. Then the Almighty caused the flow of the sea to transform. It changed direction to go partly around the Earth and the other part of the sea turned itself back leading to and encircling the land of Havilah (**Hav-vee-lah**). Now, after the flood of water, there is a beautiful clear sky and fair weather. It was most pleasant, agreeable, and appropriate to human senses. Now, after the flood, the land's glittering and precious gold metal, that is measured by weight, was beautiful. The land was ready for a good man and a good woman; even good men and good women with good words, good understanding, and good morals. As the Almighty commanded, life did come forth to life. The Almighty blessed them by His commandment saying, be fruitful, increase and grow, bring forth fruit, branch off and show fruitfulness. Conquer and subdue the Earth. Over the process of time, multiply and become many, become numerous, and do much in respect to your authority. Then, the Almighty observed them and considered. After considering, He summoned His Holy Assembly with His Voice. The Almighty preached and proclaimed to them. The Almighty spoke to them saying, from the Behemoth, I will make an Adam (**Ah-dom**). He will be a human man. He will be an individual species of the original creation of Behemoth. His species will resemble his own image and their image will represent themselves. He and his mate will bring forth children and maintain families. He and his species of persons will make themselves to be idols and their idols will be after their own nature and likeness. They will imagine themselves as being in the image of Eloheem. Their picture of Eloheem is of a supreme god who gives birth to gods, goddesses, angels, godlike ones, rulers, and great judges. Each with their own power to make divine works and each with their own special possessions. They are all false interpretations and demonic imaginations because I am the Almighty, the All Supreme Being, the All Supreme Ruler, the One True Creator of all things. Based on My Likeness to build and make patterns of design, they will be able to build and make patterns of design. I am the Almighty, the One True Living Supreme Being, based on My Likeness to adore and celebrate, they will be able to adore and celebrate. Based on My Likeness to ordain and appoint, they will be able to ordain and appoint. I will let them dominate and rule over the fish of the sea, over the fowl of the air, over the wild beasts, the cattle, the animals, and over everything that creeps and moves on the soil of the ground. Then, the Almighty finished speaking to His Holy Assembly the second time, as designated by the authority of the Almighty, for an individual monument and memorial, the name of the second flood that burst forth from the foundation of the seas is the Gihon (**Gee-hoan**). The All Supreme Being, the Creator caused this flood to go around the whole Earth and surround it. Like a skirt, it surrounded all the people of the nations that inhabited the Earth. The Almighty had caused the flow of the sea to transform. It changed direction to go partly around the Earth and the other part of the sea changed direction and turned itself back leading to and encircling the whole land of Ethiopia (**Kush**). Then, the Almighty created the first Adam (**Ah-dom**). Of mammal transformation, the Almighty shaped and formed this human being and made him come to life.

Then, of the opposite sex, for a mate, the Almighty created a female human being of mammal transformation. Then, the Almighty blessed them. He blessed them to be able to act in adoration, to be able to praise one another, to be able to kneel and give thanks, to be able to congratulate, to be able to blaspheme, and to be able to curse. He commanded them saying, by the process of time, increase and become many, multiply and become numerous. Fill your hands. Nourish and satisfy yourselves. Accomplish and replenish yourselves upon the soil of the ground in respect to the authority you are given. Your end will be in the soil of the ground. Dominate and conquer the Earth. Dominate and rule over the fish of the sea. Dominate and rule over the flying things of the air, and over every living thing that moves upon the soil of the ground. The Almighty spoke to them saying, I have given you the herb, the grass, and the green plants that have seeds. You scatter the seeds upon the Earth to sow the seed in the Earth. I have given you every tree, of timber, of firm wood, of stalk, of woody flax, and every fruit of the ground, every fruit of the tree that has seed. It is better for you and to you it will be food to eat, and the timber will be fuel for fire. I have given you all the flying things of the air, and everything that moves and creeps on the ground. I have given you all the living creatures of body, blood, and heart. Their soul is the life in their blood. I have given you dominion over all living creatures that have an activity of mind, and over all those things with desire, appetite, passions, and emotions which are the things of the soul. I have given you every green herb and every green grass for food to eat. Then, the Almighty observed everything that He made. This is the sixth miracle, the sixth work that the Almighty, the All Supreme Being, the Creator of all things completed. This is the time period from the first species of human beings to the third species of human beings. Now, all species were made to always be dependent upon the Almighty's approval. So, as the Almighty had commanded, these human beings became strong and fat. Then, they began to defile themselves. Adam (**Ah-dom**) became a hypocrite and a person of low degree. The human man chose and invited guests. He preached to them about Eloheem saying, all humans are made in the image of a god. He brought his female mate before them and proclaimed her name to be Eve (**Heh-vah**), meaning the life giver. He proclaimed her to be the mother of all living things. They created illusions that were a vain show of emptiness. The inhabitants developed and influenced extreme ways of feeding among themselves. These inhabitants cut down trees of wood to cut out and create their own qualified creator of heaven and earth. These species of human persons were deceiving hypocrites. Their hearts and minds were godlike continually. With their mind of activity and passion, after their own image and likeness, these species of human persons created metal from ore. They hammered out metal into the face of animals. They hammered out metal into the face of themselves. With feasts, they celebrated the face of animals. With feasts, they celebrated themselves as gods and goddesses. These species of human persons had very greedy appetites. They desired and enjoyed eating fresh and old raw flesh. They were always lusting for pleasure. Their rulers and judges were not humble of a low degree, but were godlike hypocrites even their common men. The All Supreme Being, the Almighty, the All Supreme Ruler observed these humans and considered. He observed them to learn about them, to see if He could respect them, and to see if He could enjoy them. The Almighty even appeared visible before them and presented Himself to them.

But The Adamites (**Ah-dom-ee**) did not make themselves servants to the Almighty. They would not labor to serve the Almighty. They would not honor and worship the Almighty. So, the Almighty judged them to be detestable. The Almighty greatly hated them even loathed them because they were stone hearted, perverse, and causing great hatred on the Earth. They hewn stone and metal to create weapons. They plummeted each other with sling stones, stones of fire, and stones of destruction, one after another at one another. They were felching meaning they were drinking semen from the genitals and sucking semen from the anus. They were being very disgusting. From among them, there came forth a great male king, a godlike one. He declared and proclaimed himself to be god in the flesh and the inhabitants made him their god. They called him their lord god. Displeased and disappointed, the Almighty condemned these low species of persons to be plucked out and put away from the region of the land and for some, to be dispersed to the end of the whole Earth because the Creator had saw all the things they did. Because of their desires, their thought and actions, the Almighty desired another, different form of human being to be an individual species of persons. The Almighty desired a species of persons that would be humble, that would care for and protect the Earth. The Creator desired a species that will worship, fulfill, and accomplish His desires. The Almighty decided to cut off the glory of those low species of human persons. He decided to cut them down and cut them out from the land, thus, mortally killing many of them. The Almighty, the All Supreme Being, the All Supreme Ruler, the Creator of all things devised a divine plan in His mind. He had preordained the birth of a different, more-humble individual species of persons. The Almighty's supreme power of seeing gave birth to the idea for an individual species Man (**Eesh**) to be created of the soil of the Earth. By His divine power of seeing, the Almighty looked onto the whole age, even onto the ending generations of this species of Man (**Eesh**). By His own divine power of seeing, the Almighty found a certain man (**Eesh**) then He considered. As the Almighty was advising Himself and looking at this man (**Eesh**)and his experiences, the Almighty gave attention to this man's mental abilities and spiritual faculties. The Almighty looked upon him joyfully and had respect for him. The Almighty continued observing His vision by His own power of seeing, now,in the sight of others, the Almighty had caused this man to appear before Himself, the Almighty. In the Almighty's Heaven, they looked at each other in the face. The Almighty found him worthy and approved this man to become of a man high degree. Of all the people, the Almighty found no one worthy but this certain man, therefore, the Almighty approved this certain man to become a great and mighty champion. The Almighty found this man worthy and approved him to become the Steward for all the Earth. At the ending generations of mankind, like the Almighty had judged the human beings of before, the All Supreme Ruler, the Creator of all things will take His Stand and execute His Judgment for His Cause. At the time of the Almighty's Judgment, a certain man will be caused to come up before the Almighty Himself. This certain man will stand before the Almighty's throne and the Almighty will approve this certain man and cause him to become of the Almighty's own divine nature. The Almighty has found this certain man worthy and will approve this certain man to be heir of the Almighty's own royalty. Then, this certain man will become the mighty ruler of earth and the steward of all mankind. The Almighty looked also onto a chosen people for Himself.

By His divine power of seeing, the Almighty found a certain people to perform His work on the Earth and these people become the Almighty's special possession on the Earth. After His Judgment of mankind and all living things, the Almighty saw good upright men on the Earth. He saw good upright women on the Earth. They all were beautiful, happy, cheerful, and prosperous. He saw them living morally good and living ethically good. The All Supreme Being saw kind men and kind women living with good understanding doing pleasant things on the Earth. With divine activity in His mind, the Almighty predetermined a resolution and pre-ordained a better species, Man (**Eesh**), to be formed with a purpose to accomplish only what He desires. With divine activity in His mind, the Creator of all things predetermined a resolution and pre-ordained a better species of persons to be formed with a purpose. When the Almighty created the Earth with its first inhabitants, the land of Earth did not include every plant. It did not include every grass. It did not include every tree nor every herb because the Almighty had not caused it to rain on the Earth. Now, the Adamites (**Ah-dom**) had not made themselves servants or worshippers to the Almighty. They would not labor to serve the Almighty. They would not honor and worship the Almighty. There was no one to till the ground. Now, the Almighty had not yet created the first Man (**Eesh**) to serve and labor for Him on the Earth. He had not yet created the first man to keep and protect His work on the Earth. The Almighty had not yet created the first man to carry out the duties of His Law and perform according to His Word. Therefore, after considering, the Almighty summoned His Holy Assembly and declared to them saying, I will make a new individual species of persons. I will create Man (**Eesh**) and of the species of man, I will create a man of high degree. He will be a great and mighty champion of the people. He will be kind and of good morals. He will be the first of his kind. He will be MY steward for the species of Man (**Eesh**). As I have set the image of the Behemoth, the species of persons of low degree, similar to them, the image of Man (**Eesh**) will resemble their own selves and their image will represent them. Each person with their own power to perform works and each person will have their own special possessions. I am the ALMIGHTY, the ONE TRUE CREATOR, based on My Likeness to build and make patterns of design, they will be able to build and make patterns of design. Based on My Likeness to adore and celebrate, they will be able to adore and celebrate. Based on My Likeness to ordain and appoint, they will be able to ordain and appoint. Based on My Likeness to think, consider, and advise; they will be able to think, consider, and advise. They will be able to act in adoration and praise one another. They will be able blaspheme and curse, but they are always dependent upon My approval. Therefore, because of the situation of the Earth, I, the Almighty, by My divine activity of mind have predetermined the creation of a species of Man and his human activity onto all his generations for the purpose of a resolution. Because of the situation of the Earth, I, the Almighty, the All Supreme Being, the All Supreme Ruler have predetermined a chosen people to be created from Man for the purpose of a resolution. Both species of Man to be formed of the Earth, both of human activity, both for the purpose of a resolution. Both are original creations. At their conception, both will be full grown individuals. Both creations of Man will be allowed to bring forth children and maintain families. I, the Almighty, the All Supreme Ruler will judge every god and goddess, every ruler and judge, every godlike and mighty one, even every person. Then, the Creator sent out a command from His voice.

With flashing lightning about, there came a mist of vapor and water onto the Earth. This watered the entire face of the Earth and caused the first down pouring rain that the low species of human persons had seen on the Earth. For the third time, as designated by the authority of the Almighty, for an individual monument and memorial, the name for the third flood that came from the sea is Hiddekel (**He-del-lakh**). At the birth of the Almighty's concept, at the idea of Him creating (**Eesh**) Man, when counted, it is threescore and fifteen years, therefore, at the command that comes from the Almighty, He caused a flood of water to break out from the flowing sea and spread forward toward various places to disperse and drown the low species of human beings to their end. As a whirl, the flood came rapidly from the sea onto the talebearers, onto those who maliciously gossip their own manner of living. It came onto those perverse and boasting in their own behavior. The flood came onto those that did not depart away from gender copulation with animals of four legs. The flood came rapidly from the sea even onto the weak, onto the traveling person, onto those at ease, and onto those exercising themselves. The rushing flood entered Eastward against Assyria. The flood spread more and more. A fourth part of the children even of the great grandchildren died from the flood that broke forth from the rushing Euphrates. Their male king was the highest rank and mightiest among the low species of human persons. He discerned the weather activity and departed away. He escaped to the tip top of a mountain summit in that land. When the flood came in from the flowing sea, he heard his people petrified in terror even crying out his name. As their god, they called out to him and he saw the people from a distance. His families, his kinsman, his country men were sinking in the water as a motionless stone. Every habitation for his nation was dispersed to the ends of the Earth or drowned to their end. When the flood water proceeded back to the flowing sea, shaking his head, the male king saw the heap of debris and rubbish on the land and condemned the commandment sent from the Almighty, the All Supreme Being, the All Supreme Ruler, the Creator of all things. After the flood of Hiddekel, when the water proceeded back to the flowing sea, there was no good water for the species of (**Eesh**) man to drink in gulps. Now, man (**Eesh**) had not yet been formed, but was preordained to be the husband of the land and there was no water to supply and irrigate the land. There was no fresh water for the husband of the land to wash himself. The Almighty did not want the habitat for man (**Eesh**) after he had been created to fall and fail. With the purpose to deliver delight to the first habitat for the species of man, with the purpose to deliver prosperity and pleasantness to the region, the Creator commanded the underground streams of flowing water to rise. The Creator caused a variant, a different form of water to come forth. Suddenly, from the shaking ground, the underground streams of water within the Earth rose through the soil and proceeded to the surface of the ground and appeared in a garden. Then, water came out into the garden and expanded, forming a stream through the garden and proceeded out into the field, then, into the land, then into the region, into the country, then, into the flowing sea. Now there was fresh water for the preordained husband of the land to wash himself and to drink in gulps. Now, there was water to supply and irrigate the garden, the land, even the face of the Earth.

From the garden, a stream of water departed through the field, then proceeded out into the land, onto the side of a flowing river, that proceeded to two rivers, then dividing and expanding into four parts, then going through the mountain pass and into the flowing sea. As a potter molds clay into a form, shaking the whole Earth, the Almighty formed a specific land for a country. It was a land of mountain ranges and hills that goes against the sea. It was hereon the Earth where the Almighty created and established (**Eesh**) Man. During the time for reviving green vegetation, the Almighty revived the land of the living with fresh flowing water. The Creator renewed the soil. The green vegetation began sprouting. On the earth and in the land, the Almighty caused plants and herbs to sprout and bud abundantly thick again. He caused vegetation to sprout with sweet aromas. Then the Creator brought forth a supernatural phenomenon and caused the stalks of flax to accelerate their own growth and they did spring forth. He caused the trees to spring up and grow branches. Every firm wood tree sprouted up and grew branches. He caused fruit trees to sprout up and produce sweet, delightful food to eat. The All Supreme Being, the Creator of all things caused this growth to thickly surround a small piece of land and it was like a garden: the stalks of flax for fiber material and the timber from trees to perform carpentry. The Almighty renewed the community of quick running animals. He renewed the strong beasts that move as troops. He revived the multitude of springing insects and moving things, but He did not revive the former creatures nor the former animals, nor the former things that had an appetite to destroy life. He did not restore the things that desired to eat fresh or old raw flesh. This was so the male human from the low species could not use them to attack nor cause a creature, wild animal, or beast to have an appetite for fresh or raw old flesh. Beneath the luminous bodies and blazing light of the stars, beneath the celestial bodies of element, beneath the sky, beneath the atmosphere where the clouds move, the Almighty, the Creator of all things revived the fowl of the air. He renewed the flying birds that have their wings covered with feathers and the winged insects. The All Supreme Being looked onto the ground with favor and caused the land to be rich, beautiful, pleasant, and precious to His sight. Now, it was pleasant for Him to delight Himself in. The land was made agreeable to the fragile nature and the physical senses of a good upright man and a good upright woman. Then, as a potter shapes clay, the Almighty formed the body of the first Man (**Eesh**) with the clay of the Earth. The Almighty cannot lose His Life by giving His Life away. He cannot be murdered. He cannot be killed. The Almighty blew a life energy into the nose of the Man and the Man's body began to rise. His skin formed and his blood formed. The Almighty caused a blast of wind to blow air into the man's body. As the body began breathing, the Almighty formed his appetites, his inspirations, his thoughts, his emotions, his passions, his pleasures, and his desires to be the same as the soul of an animal or breathing creature. These are the things of the soul, and the soul is the life in the blood of man. Now, the man was a living being. This was the seventh miracle, the seventh work the Almighty completed. The first Man (**Eesh**) was created fair, dark, and his face showed a healthy red from the flow of his blood. Enclosed by trees, surrounded by a thick growth of plants and herbs, the Almighty appeared before the Man. As they looked at each other in the face, the Almighty spoke and commanded saying, I am the ALMIGHTY, the ALL SUPRME BEING. I am the All Supreme Ruler.

I am the most powerful being and the most holy being. I, alone, am self-existing. I, alone, am everlasting. Beware, you can freely eat the fruit from every tree in the land, but you will look away from the wooden book of knowledge that gives you understanding and perception of good and evil. Do not let your eyes observe the contents in the wooden book of knowledge that is in the garden. You will not read the contents in it. The book is fastened and is firmly shut. In the day that you read from it, you will certainly die before your time. The Almighty continued speaking to the Man saying, you have charge of the land. You will take care of the land and protect it. To save your life, you must obey My command and you must stay within the bounds of My command. Now, beware and wait for My command. The Man presented himself humbly and was divinely inspired by the Almighty. The Man was obedient and with passion, the Man began performing the charge that came from the Almighty. He committed himself to honor the command sent from the Almighty, the All Supreme Being, the All Supreme Ruler. The Man became a special possession performing a special work to honor the Almighty. Then, the Almighty caused the animals of the land to come to the Man and they dwelled with him. The Man observed them, discerned them, and distinguished them. The Man followed them, inspected them, and fed them. The Man was gaining experience as he learned about these animals' passions, desires, appetites, emotions, their activity of mind and their will. The Almighty wanted him to decide for himself whether to approve of them or determine they are suspicious in character and cannot be trusted. The man learned to respect the species of Behemoth and the animals of the land. The Manchose his favorites.

The Man named the species of Behemoth and appointed them reputation, honor, authority, and glory. Every living being with a soul in its blood and every creeping thing that the Creator brought before the Man, the Man called their name out aloud and appointed them a reputation. With great delight, the Almighty relaxed on His Throne. In His own Heaven, all the Almighty's Holy Assembly kneeled before Him. They greatly praised the Almighty and they greatly congratulated Him. They worshipped the Almighty because He is the All Supreme Ruler. He is the Creator of all things. They shouted out praises to Him. They adored the miracles He had shown them. As they celebrated before the Almighty, they blessed the Almighty one toward another saying, the Almighty is the most powerful. He alone is everlasting. The Almighty is the most holy. He alone everlasting. With great delight, in front of His Holy Assembly, the Almighty took a Perfect Oath to increase honor to Himself. The Almighty took, as it is called, a Seventh Oath to increase the honor to Himself. The Almighty took a Seventh Oath to increase the honor to Himself because He had completed the creation of His Earth and the Earth's Heavens to His satisfaction. He took a Seventh Oath to increase the honor to Himself because He created a species of persons worthy of becoming a special possession to Himself. This Oath is forever binding and it will forever keep the Earth, its Heavens, and its species of Man established. Then, the Almighty declared and commanded His Seventh Oath to be observed as a memorial, a monument, and a remembrance forever. And all these things were recorded. At the sign of life, the male king from the low species, a hypocrite, the Adamite (**Ah-dom**) of the species of Behemoth had come into the same territory. Spying, the male human stared at the Man (**Eesh**) and considered.

As the male human was advising himself, he saw the Man (**Eesh**) had a merry spirit and the Man was full of life. The Man appeared very strong and active. Afterwards of that time, the Man was quickly running through a field in the land. Spying, the male saw the face of the Man and the male gazed at the cheerful countenance on the Man's face. At this exact time, the Man saw the face of the male, and the Man looked at him. As they looked at each other in the face, the male began to move toward the man to challenge him. The male was longsuffering and breathing rapidly from his nose. The male had an angry countenance on his face. The male desired the Almighty to disesteem His new creation. The male lusted for the Almighty to lose respect for His new creation. The male was visualizing any way he could cause a bad reputation to be applied to the Man. In his inner being, in his soul, there was a wildly strong passion to bring his own wrath upon the Man. The male intended to kill the Man dead. In this place, at this instant, the Man had an encounter with the male person of the low species. The same species of humans that the Almighty loathes. After their encounter, the Man called out and declared the name of that male person. The Man named him the Adversary. In a land that has hills and mountain ranges against the sea, on a plain that runs against mountains, in a field on that plain, in a garden of that field, a garden that became the home of wild animals, there, the man rested. The Almighty summoned His Holy Assembly. He spoke to them openly and made a promise to them on His own reputation. The Almighty spoke to them, saying, I will judge the male person, the hypocrite who is a godlike one. He is exiled and sentenced to condemnation. He is sentenced to be alone. He is sentenced to be haunted by torment, but even at this place and time, he continues to act proudly against My command. The Man is humble and upright, but this male is trying cause the Man to fall out of My happiness by sin. I will favor the Man. He has kept My charge and is performing My special work, but that male is trying to cause the man to fall out of My grace. This male person is a hypocrite who speaks very proudly. He acts very boldly and he believes in boasting in himself. He desires to challenge My command. This male human is very annoying and certainly makes Me angry. This Adversary has attacked the Man and tried to overwhelm him. This Adversary attempted to capture My special possession. The Man did not surrender. He was not captured, but he is losing his energy of hope. The Man has fallen away, alone, to himself. The Almighty continued speaking openly to His Holy Assembly saying, after I long suffer, I will answer the Adversary's challenge openly and directly. I will win with the most glorious victory. At the end of the age, when I command the term of the age to be finished, then suddenly, I will answer him completely. I will fulfill My judgment. Also, I will judge against all hypocrites and against all those that are godlike. I will judge against all gods and every goddess. I will judge against all the rulers, all the judges, all the mighty persons, and all the common persons that come into being from his semen. It will come true. At the end of the whole age, I will judge all mankind. At the end of the whole age, of My own promise, I have appointed a humble workman to put My doctrine in order. Then, I will bring this certain Man of My own promise forth and cause him to stand as a mighty warrior. I will establish him as the Steward of Mankind. He will govern all mankind. I will bring forth certain upright men and I will cause them to stand as mighty warriors.

I will bring forth certain upright women and I will cause them to stand as mighty warriors. Altogether, organized as a unit, I will cause them to invade the lands of the Earth. Altogether, they will execute My judgment against hypocrites and against liars. They will execute My judgment against any person that proudly speaks against My name, My reputation, My honor, My glory, or My command. They will execute My judgment against anyone that avouches for a liar or lying report about My name, My reputation, My honor, My glory, or My command. They will execute My judgment against any individual that pays wages to declare a lying report about My name, My reputation, My honor, My glory, or My command. They will execute My judgment against any individual that asks for wages to declare a lying report about My name, My reputation, My honor, My glory, or My command. They will execute My judgment against any individual that takes advantage of a person by speaking lies or laboring for lies about My name, My reputation, My honor, My glory, or My command. They will execute My judgment against any individual that takes another person's money by speaking lies or laboring for lies about My name, My reputation, My honor, My glory, or My command. I will throw them all down and smite them all out. The Almighty continued speaking, saying, it not a good thing for Man to be alone. It would be a good thing and it will be appropriate to Me to bring him forth a mate so the Man will not be alone. I will create a (**Nek-kay-vah**) Woman. With longer hair, the Woman(**Nek-kay-vah**) will be fair in the man's sight. She will help him and support him. The Man will think to go one way or the other and she will follow to help him. The Woman will help the Man to accomplish and advance in his purpose because she is comparable to his intellect. The Man will be joyful in his companion's presence because his mate is created kind, humble, pleasant, and honest. Together, they will serve My cause and they will labor according to My command. Like the Man, this Woman(**Nek-kay-vah**)will be full grown at her conception. She will be able to bring forth children for the species of mankind, therefore, Woman is appointed to be the Man's mate. When the Man (**Eesh**) and Woman (**Nek-kay-vah**) join their bodies together, they will become one flesh. Then they are married, the Woman is now (**Ish-shah**). Of the Man's semen, of the Man's lineage, I will bring forth a certain Son. This certain Son will repair My name, My reputation, My honor, My authority, and My glory. He will put My Report in order and build up My name and My Reputation with honor and glory. Therefore, I have assigned this first Man's inheritance to that certain Son of his lineage because this first Man will transgress against My command. In this place, the Man's mate, the Woman, who is naïve, who is humble, kind, and honest will be caused to become an adulteress like the quarrelsome female Eve (**Hav-vah**) of the species of Behemoth. Like a house being built up from its foundation, the Woman will be built up to become the mother of a family by the Adversary. Her desire and emotions will be built up and preyed upon by the Adversary. Because of the Adversary, the Woman will cause the Man to lose his inheritance. By his charm and conduct, the Adversary will lead the Woman, and cause her to follow him alone. Then, she will fall into the hands of the Adversary. The Adversary will be very overwhelming by throwing himself upon her. They will sexually lie together and he will plant his seed. Through the Woman, the Adversary who has been cast into exile will restore his children.

Then, the hypocrite will be set free of his bondage. His child with the Woman will become a fugitive, but will also have children. The Woman will have a second son. This son is by the Man, of his semen, of his lineage. Because of her actions, the Woman will be given the custom of the female species of Behemoth and she will die before her time. At the end of the whole age, I, the Almighty, will judge all mankind, then I will cause the Adversary's glory to fall short and his seed will fall a violent death. I will judge the Adversary who will mingle himself into the species of mankind. I will judge all of his persons that come into being through mankind. When I judge every living person of mankind, I will assign the Man's certain Son his lot, when I assign the Man's certain Son his inheritance, then I will send this Son, who has become My own Son, to attack all the enemy. Altogether, with this certain Son, I will gather certain upright men and certain upright women from mankind. I will assign them their inheritance, then I will send them to take vengeance against all the enemy. The enemy will be killed one by one and one after the other until they perish away. All those persons that are like this adversary will rot and waste away. The Almighty finished speaking to His Holy Assembly, then there were flashes of lightning in the valley and the Almighty caused a deep sleep to fall upon the Adversary. As the Adversary remained asleep a long time, the Almighty punished him and the Adversary's skin began to form of leprosy. The Almighty closed up the route and shut up in the way into the garden. The Almighty caused a deep sleep to fall upon the Man. As the Man was sleeping, the Almighty formed a Woman(**Nek-kay-vah**) from the clay of the Earth. After the ALMIGHTY created the Woman's body, He took out one curbed rib from the man's body. He repaired the rib taken out of the Man's body and closed up his flesh. Then, the Almighty carried the rib He had taken out of the Man's body to the Woman's body. The Almighty fixed the Man's rib into the body of the Woman and closed up her flesh. The Woman is now of the Man's flesh by the rib she received from him. Before the Woman received the Man's rib, she did not have any blood relation to the species of Man, so she could not be included in a being a pure person of his species, nor could she be included in the Seventh Oath taken by the ALMIGHTY to increase honor to Himself by giving mankind permanent possession of the Earth, but now by this event, she had been brought into the blood lineage of Man. Now, she is a part in the portion of the Almighty's everlasting Covenant which is the Seventh Oath. The rib taken from the Man and given to the Woman caused her to be directed related by blood to the Man. Now, by blood, she is bound to the species of Mankind. She is forbidden to copulate and conceive outside the species of Mankind. Apart from the Man, the Woman cannot exist as her own individual species of persons. After the Woman became a living being with a soul, a short time had passed. The Man was sitting in the garden and lightning flashed about the land, the Man was counting the highest corners of the anvil clouds that were in the sky. As follows, he was counting, one, two, three, thus, one after the other at this repetition by the order he saw the clouds. Then, the Almighty caused the Woman to wander into the garden to be introduced to the Man. From a distance, she was merry. She was happy. She was beautiful. The Man came into a trance and stared at her skin even the nakedness of her body. He observed her for a time then he considered. He uttered to himself, saying, this one is not self-boasting like the Adversary who acted proudly.

This one is not like the Adversary who openly spoke against my Creator and commanded me to challenge him. This one does not have the flesh of animals nor does this one have a genital organ as an animal. This one's footsteps is not the sound of a hoof beat, but this one's feet are the same as mine. This one walks the same way I do. I am strong fleshed and this one is lean fleshed. This one's body has the selfsame skin, the same body limbs, and the same kind of hands as I do. This one's genital organ looks opposite to fit with mine. So, our bodies can become one flesh together. Certainly after such a thing, the two would be joined together and become a family. This one is a female but not the female gender of the species of Behemoth. This one is alone with no other living being from any other species with her. In his heart, the Man told himself saying, this one is the same bone of my bones and the same flesh as my flesh. Indeed, the Man was happy about this occurrence. This female became precious to the man. The Man thought about what to say and considered how to declare a name for the female. Then, he called out aloud and invited the female to meet him. She did approach man and drew near to him. After the encounter, the Man chose and invited guests to preach to them and proclaim to them. The Man spoke aloud saying, no one can be free from their bond to the Almighty. Everything is of His own creation. To the Almighty, you are either His slave, His worshipper, or His servant. Nothing can help free you from your bond to the Almighty. A good person, whether he is a champion or a person of high degree, whether he is a husband or servant, a good person will respect and honor the Almighty, the All Supreme Being, the All Supreme Ruler, the Creator of all things. A good person will not turn away from the Almighty. The Man continued speaking, saying this person beside me is the same bone of my bones and the same flesh as my flesh. This person is chosen to be named Woman (**Nek-kay-vah**). She has been appointed and reserved for Man. She is my helper. By the command sent from the Almighty, she is to support and care for Man. Therefore, I select and choose this female I call Woman who is of my own species. I accept her to be my own family and she is reserved for my possession. A man that is alone in life will acquire a woman to start a family of his own. Therefore, for a woman to be a wife (**Ish-shah**), for a woman to be married to a Man, a Man will leave his father's household and from under his mother's care. He will cling to the woman he has acquired. He will keep her close to him and follow her closely. Together, they will become one flesh, then they are to be considered joined together as a family. The Woman has become the man's wife and she is the man's possession. They will not leave off from their marriage. The woman will cleave to the man. She will not leave him empty nor leave him alone. The man and the woman will help each other, support each other, and care for each other as a family. In this manner, in this way, every man, every woman, and every family will repeat and follow the Almighty's command as honest, correct, and true. With no confusion, the man and the woman were naked before one another and were not troubled by the reason of their own nakedness. The man and the woman were not hesitating because of their nudity. The man was not disappointed at the nakedness of the woman neither was the woman disappointed at the nakedness of the man. They did not feel shame or disgrace because the man and the woman did not have thoughts to cause them shame. There was no cause for them to act shameful. Now, the Adversary is an adulterer. He is a hypocrite. He is an enchanter who practiced and learned to whispers magic spells.

He carefully observes omens and practices fortunetelling. He uses enchantments and practices divinations. He believes his soul is of a serpent constellation. He imagines his inner being to be a great dragon. He pictures himself to be a quickly moving dragon. For attacking the Man, for attempting to take possession of the Man, and for the sin he committed by acting proud against the command sent from the Almighty; the Almighty struck the male human with a spreading skin disease of leprosy. To be for a sign, the Almighty struck the male with a second spreading skin disease of serpigo. Now, struck by two spreading skin diseases one after the other, the Adversary formed beyond what was normal. The Adversary had become disturbed, confused, and ashamed in his mind. In a dry and empty place of the valley with spotted, pale, rough, irregular skin, his hope and expectation was beginning to fail. He had no female to be his adulteress wife. He had no family of his own. Then, the Adversary, the enchanter arose from his resting place. Now, the Adversary was very clever in wickedness. He was very cautious using his trickery. The Adversary was strong and more wicked in his self-cunning than any beast, any animal, or living creature in the field of the Earth. After the Almighty led the Woman to Man. The Woman and the Man continued to observe one another. They continued to eat together. They had become very close. Then, the Almighty appeared before them, as the Man and Woman were looking at the Almighty, the Almighty spoke and commanded saying, I am the Almighty, the All Supreme Being, the All Supreme Ruler, the Creator of all things. I am the Most Powerful and I am the Most Holy. Beware, you can freely eat the fruit from every tree in the land, but you will look away from the wooden book of knowledge that gives you understanding and perception of good and evil. Do not let your eyes observe the contents in the wooden book of knowledge that is in the garden. You will not read the contents in it. The book is fastened and is firmly shut. In the day that you read from it, you will certainly die before your time. The Almighty continued speaking to the them saying, the Man has charge of the land. Together, you will take care of the land and protect it. To save your lives, you must obey My command and you must stay within the bounds of My command. Now, beware and wait for My command. The Man and the Woman presented themselves humbly and was divinely inspired by the Almighty. Then, the Almighty caused them to become busy. By their ears, they heard the voice and command from the Almighty. Together, they committed to honor and serve the Almighty as HIS servants and worshippers. The Almighty caused them to become industrious and perform His righteousness. He set a work for them to perform. The man fashioned tools to build. He used tools to hedge thorns that spring up about the garden. Together, the man and the woman were performing the command that came from the Almighty. The Man had stored the commandment in his memory even about the everlasting Covenant. The Man laid down earth and stone for an altar to worship the Almighty. Together, the man and woman set up a foundation for a house. They built a floor with thin planks of timber from a tree then they set up thin planks of timber for the sides of the house. They set up thin planks of timber for a ceiling and even set up a door to fill the doorway. The Almighty caused them to continue working and they were being industrious. Not many days after, after he had finished eating, the man rested, then he fell asleep. While in his sleep, he had a vision.

He saw a humble servant and considered. As he was gazing at this humble servant, he was observing. This humble servant was different than any man of the men of Mankind. He saw this humble man be brought up to meet the Almighty and He saw the Almighty choose this Man as being worthy. Then, the Almighty caused this certain Man to become a mighty champion. He saw the Almighty cause this certain Man to become a man of high degree and this certain Man became a Steward for all Mankind. As the man was sleep in his vision, the Adversary was spying the land. He saw the woman walking not far from the garden and he desired her. Staring at her, he considered and determined what to say. Acting proudly, he presented himself to the woman. Speaking against the Almighty, he asked the woman her name, then he asked saying, has your god commanded you not to eat the birds that devour the fruit in the trees? Has you god told you not to destroy flesh? The Adversary continued speaking to her by asking, have you promised your god not to read from the wooden book for knowledge and perception of good and evil? The woman answered by saying, we cannot destroy nor can we oppress living flesh. We cannot eat the birds that devour the fruit of the trees. We cannot use the sword to kill the beasts to eat for food. We cannot waste the trees by destroying them with fire, but we can use the wood from the trees for building. We can eat the fruit on the ground and the fruit of the trees, but we cannot read from the wooden book that is among us in the center of the garden. The Almighty told us to beware. He commanded us not open the wooden book for knowledge and perception of good and evil. He commanded us not come near to reach onto it, in no wise, unless as a penalty, we die before our time. As they were speaking, the Adversary determined this female was not of his species. She was the mate of the Man. Now, he intended to destroy the seed of Mankind. He planned to make the woman become an adulteress. The Adversary desired for the Man to become as himself, an adulterer. In his heart, the Adversary spoke to himself saying, surely together I will cause the man and woman to be put to death. Acting proudly and in his own self-boasting, the Adversary challenged the Woman. He challenged the command that comes from the voice of the Almighty. The Adversary spoke to the Woman saying, surely your penalty will not be death. You are a special work and a special possession to your god. Your god has this knowledge and He understands. In the time that you read the wooden book of knowledge and perception of good and evil you will become extremely wise. You will become godlike. You will be a better living being. You will become a goddess. Your eyes will be able to see what you cannot see. You will be able to live with extraordinary mental and spiritual qualities. Out a fountain of water, you will see your appearance more cheerful and beautiful. You will be able to eat the birds that devour the fruit in the trees. For food, you will be able to use the sword to kill the beasts. You will be happy feeding on the richest of flesh, the best of every kind. Your eye will tell you what is unpleasant and evil. You will be able to discern and find out what is hurtful, and you will remain a special possession to your god. Then, the Adversary asked, has your god told you the reward for becoming a bride. Do you know the benefits of being a family and having children? Has your god commanded you not to be fruitful and bring forth children? Self-boasting, he continued speaking to the woman saying, I swear and certify the goodness of the reward that comes from having children.

Furthermore, your god can certainly acknowledge the precious pleasantness of becoming acquainted with the flesh of a person. Sexually lying down with a man is very agreeable to the pleasure senses. It is the right way to learn by experience. You get the right understanding by experience. In sex, you will bring forth a beautiful family and great kinsman. With respect to your god, me, as a man of skill, I will make it known to you. From the wooden book, I will teach you how to lay with a man if you promise to experience this with me, and use what you have learned to teach the Man. As the Almighty had foretold his Holy Assembly now was the time for fate to befall upon the woman. Alone together, the woman and the Adversary arrived at the center of the garden. Among the fruit and trees, in the warmth of the day, ignorant and unaware, the woman rebelled against the Almighty's command. By the cunning speech from the Adversary, the woman became disobedient to the command that comes from the Almighty. The Adversary reached out and took hold of the book. When the woman saw the wooden book she considered. The book looked beautiful in her sight and she wanted to learn about it. By the cunning speech of the Adversary, she believed it to be a book most desired. She believed the book would make her extremely wise. She imagined herself becoming godlike. She pictured herself becoming a goddess. Very suddenly, it happened. The Adversary did not waste time. He laid his hand upon the woman and made her lie down, then he joined to the woman becoming one flesh with her. As she was reading, she had gained perception of good and evil. As the woman and the Adversary were indulging and the Adversary was secreting his semen, the woman's eyes were opened. Now, she knew she was naked and helpless. She could see that she was naked and helpless. She looked at the Adversary and judged his appearance. She became displeased. The Adversary became angry and violently struck the ground. The woman became unhappy with what was happening and began crying aloud. The Adversary withdrew among the trees and thick plants of the garden. Indeed, this happened as the man slept. This happened as the man was observing a vision of a certain Man the Almighty found worthy. This certain Man became a mighty champion. This certain Man became a person of high degree and this certain Man was appointed to be the Steward for all mankind. Suddenly, the man awoke from the sound of weeping in the garden. As he got closer to the sound of weeping, he found the woman weeping aloud. He came near to her and showed care for her. As soon as the Man came to her, she offered him the book. She put the book into his hands, then she gave him her body. The man consented and willingly gave his body to her. Now, the woman had become sexually acquainted with both the man and the Adversary. She is as an adulteress. At a fountain of water, the man and the woman looked at their color and appearance. They were content and felt pleased. Then, they acknowledged they were naked and in need. Next, they did what they thought best to do. To cover their loins, they sewed together growing leafage and sprouting vines so their waists could be covered. As they were singing, joking, and lacking seriousness, they heard thunder crackling as the sound of a very loud instrument so they listened with interest. Then a familiar voice called out them saying, come to Me and listen. Through the trees, the plants, and the stick stalks of vegetation that familiar voice moved through the garden as if it was being carried by the wind.

First, the voice was light then as a cry aloud. At hearing the voice cry aloud, the Adversary hid himself in the deepness of thick vegetation. The man and the woman paid attention and considered. They spoke to one another saying that is the voice of the Almighty. It is He who judges every god and every goddess. He is summoning us. The man and woman in fear decided to hide themselves in the thick stalks of vegetation. Then, the voice of the Almighty asked aloud saying, "Man, where are you?" In his heart, the man thought about what to say, then he came forth from out the thick vegetation to answer to the command. As the man stood before the voice of the Almighty, he spoke saying, "I heard thunder crackling as the sound of a very loud instrument. I heard a voice and I believed the sound of it was familiar." The voice called out saying, "Come to Me and listen." Then, with the blast of the wind, the voice became a loud call. I stand in fear. I am naked and helpless before you, out of respect and honor, I hid myself. The Almighty spoke to the man saying, you understand you are naked and helpless. You have read from the book of knowledge and perception of good and evil. By His desire, at the Almighty's command, the weather in that region of the sky displayed His power. A tempest, a whirlwind, a violent and windy storm appeared. The SPIRIT of the Almighty appeared visible. The SPIRIT of the Almighty was agitated and angry. The Almighty was in the seat of His emotions. Animated of energy, His SPIRIT was inhaling and exhaling like a person strongly breathing. In his heart, the man thought about what to say. Then, the man spoke saying, I awoke when I heard a loud noise in the garden. I heard the woman weeping aloud. I am a humble man not a fighting warrior type. I came to her to comfort her. I came to her to care for her. The woman you gave me offered me the book. She put the book into my hands and gave me her body. I did read about eating flesh for food. I did read about using weapons to kill. I did read about bringing children forth to have a family. I did read the book with her and we indulged in the pleasure of our bodies. The Almighty spoke to the woman saying, I commanded you not to read the book of knowledge and perception of good and evil. You are ordained to be with the man. You do not know what you have done, but I know what you have done. Answer Me. I command you to speak. In her heart, the woman considered what to say. The woman answered the Almighty saying, the enchanter came to me acting very proud. He challenged me and Your command. I did not discern what his cunning speech offered. I did not discern what his promising words offered. He certified himself of Your command. I did not think about his desire neither did I challenge him. I read the book of knowledge and perception of good and evil with him. I did read about eating flesh for food. I read about using fire and weapons to kill. I did read about bringing forth children to have a family. The enchanter fed on my desires and seduced me. He corrupted my way of thinking and he completely deceived me. Then, the Almighty summoned the enchanter and the enchanter was before Him. The Almighty spoke to him, saying, this place, this period of time, this day has been recorded and so will all the days of this age until the end of age at the time of trouble. Because you have done this, being committed to challenge My command because you have done this, putting in order a plan to turn My creation against Me because you have done this, you have revived your community. You have restored your kingdom.

The Almighty continued speaking to the Adversary saying, onto this enchanter, who whispers enchantments and uses magic spells, onto this enchanter who believes his soul is of the serpent constellation. Onto this enchanter who imagines his inner being to be a great serpent, onto this enchanter who pictures himself to be a quickly moving dragon, onto this enchanter who is formed beyond what is normal, you are laid under a bitter curse and you will be made to be bitter curse. You are cursed more than all the species of Behemoth because the children of your semen will devour all flesh. Whether of birds, whether of beasts, whether of humans, whether of things that do not move, the children of your semen will consume it. They will kill with the sword. They will use fire to destroy. They will be as a pestilence. They will be like calamity. They will devour by oppression and they will freely pulverized the earth. As mortar is used to ground things into powder, rubbish, debris, ashes, and ore will be what is left over from their devouring. Your lineage and the congregations that are of your passion, desire, and appetite will eat with joy all the days of their lives, all the days of the age, until the end of the age, in the required season, at the day of trouble and troubled weather. As for now, I have put hatred and hostility between you and the woman (**Ish-shah**). I have put hatred and hostility between you and the man. I will put hatred and hostility between your child and the man's child. I will put hatred and hostility between your descendants and the man's descendants. At the end of the age, at that time, I, the Almighty, will put an active hatred and hostility between the seed of your semen and the women of mankind. At the end of the age, at that time, I will put an active hatred and hostility between the seed of your semen and the men of mankind. At the end of the age, at that time, My practitioner of righteousness, whose mark is of bruised heels, will hate your posterity and all those who lie in wait. Your ghost will snap at his footsteps and desire to destroy his journey. Your posterity will cover his foot prints so that no one can follow him, yet at the end, He will overwhelm all your armies. He will crush your highest leader, your highest priest, then He will crush all your leaders of the nations. All your cities and all your leaders of men will be crushed. At the last part when, I, the Almighty take My stand to perform My judgment upon mankind. Beginning with your best nation, whose height is at the stars, I will impose My hostility upon them. I will cause My practitioner of righteousness and those that are of his nation to crush your posterity's kingdom. They will seize the cities, the priests, the families, and those of the poor that have the soul and mind of an animal. All kingdoms will be invaded, overwhelmed, knocked down, and overthrown, but your kingdom, your posterity's kingdom will perish forever. I will command for every person that comes from the semen you have sowed to be killed. I will command for every person that is of your moral quality to be put to death and they will be left dead to rot away. A fetus of your semen is in the woman. This fetus will labor and break forth from its source in her belly. When your body of flesh is dead, your soul will become a ghost. Now, you depart away from here and live your life. You go your own way and follow your own manner of living. The Almighty spoke to the woman saying, you are an adulteress. You have conceived and become pregnant with a child by adulterer and you conceived again and become pregnant with a child by your husband.

Over the process of time, as the gender of your species multiplies in number and grows to become many, as the gender of your species continues to multiply and becomes exceedingly great in number, you will transgress against ME greatly by doing much in respect to the Adversary and his archers. They are those that set traps. They are those who sit and wait to shoot and wound. You will do much in respect to those who teach others how to lay snares. Therefore, as the gender of your species multiplies in number, I will also multiply their worries greatly. They will multiply their idols greatly. I will multiply the pain of their body and mind. Their ability to conceive will be grievous to their body and mind. Their pregnancy will grievous to their body and mind. When they bring forth children it will hurt of pain and distress. I, the Almighty, will cause them to need help bringing forth children and their pregnancy will be devised and contrived. They will idolize bringing forth children and they will idolize themselves as the object of creation. Over time, the craving of a man for a woman and the desire of a woman for a man that I have appointed will be devoured by the Adversary. Then, the craving of a man for a woman and the desire of a woman for a man will become very different from what I have appointed. This is the desire that will reign and exercise dominion until the end of the age. Therefore, I will multiply all their hardships and sorrows greatly. The Almighty continued speaking to the woman saying, you will give birth for that human who is of an animal. You will give birth to his son. His son will be a son of injustice. He will be of wicked behavior. He will transgress against Me and bring forth iniquity. Right after your firstborn is born, you will give birth again. You will give birth to a son for the man. This son will be of MY righteousness. Of these two persons, the man is your husband and you are his possession. The man is My servant and he will rule over you. From the man's lineage, I have ordained a certain people. I have appointed these certain people to serve and worship Me. From the Man's lineage, I have ordained a certain Son. I have anointed this certain Son because he alone is worthy to be MY OWN SON. Born in servitude, I will bring Him up among the stranger, the rebel, and the robber, but I will support Him and keep Him within the bounds of My command. He will restore My name. He will repair My reputation, My honor, My glory, and My Word. Then, I will cause Him to become a champion of the people. I will cause Him to become a man of high degree. I will make Him have dominion and ruling power over all mankind and over all the Earth. I will cause Him to become the Steward for mankind. In respect to the people I have ordained to serve and worship ME, in respect to the certain Son I will bring forth to become My own, you will not perish. Then, the Almighty spoke to the man saying, now, you heard weather. You listened thunder crackling as a loud instrument. You heard My familiar voice call out aloud saying, come to me and listen. You listened as My familiar voice moved through the garden along with the blast of wind through the stalks and plants of the garden. First, My voice was light then, as a call aloud. You understood My language, but you did not answer Me. You determined it was My familiar voice summoning you, but instead of answering Me, you and the woman rebelled and hid among the trees and the plants in the garden. I told you to beware and consider. I commanded you not to open the wooden book of knowledge and perception of good and evil. I commanded you not to read the contents of the book. Because you submitted to the crying report from the woman who became one flesh with the Adversary as a man married to a woman.

Because you accepted her plea and agreed to her request to read the contents of the book. Because you did not discern the idol woman and obey My commandment. I have made you to be a bitter curse and have caused you and your descendants to carry this bitter curse everyday continually until the end. The soil of the land even all the surface of the Earth is cursed because of you. The Earth will grow prickly thorns and sprout out useless plants to you. Now, I will cause you to freely kill with the sword and use fire to destroy flesh. I will cause you to freely eat the flesh of birds and beasts. I will cause your work to be painful and extremely hard. You will be devoured by it all the days for your life. You will waste away in it all the days for your life. It will consume you away until the days for your life are no more. You will eat your food after you sweat from hard labor. You will sweat and perspire on your face and nose during your labor. I will cause you to eat sorrow and misfortune. I will cause you to eat disappointment and loss. I will cause you will eat suffering and oppression. I will cause you to eat from anything and everything in every manner to its totality. You and your descendants will eat from all these things daily and yearly continually all they days of your life even all of mankind until the time for trouble in the end when all mankind will hear My Case and My Cause. You and your descendants will be angry a long time, until, you return into the Earth. From the Earth you were formed and to the Earth you will return. The Almighty continued speaking to the man saying, for your sin, I am displeased, but of your lineage, I have preordained a humble workman who I have found worthy to become My own Son. It will come true. At the very end of the age, He will put My report in order, and I will prepare him. I will bring Him to meet Me, then make Him a fighting man warrior-like and mighty. He will commit to perform and accomplish My command only. He will execute My judgment. The Almighty continued speaking to the man, and commanded him, saying, as at other times, this day has been written and recorded and each day hereafter. Tomorrow at sunrise, you will begin a working day, a twenty-four-hour period. From sunrise to sunset, there will be a space of time for the warm to hot hours of the day, followed by a space of time from sunset to sunrise, for the coolness of the evening and night. Within this process of time, you will work and journey to become industrious. This process of time is appointed and fixed for the whole age of mankind every day continually until the time for trouble in the end when all mankind will hear My Case and My Cause. Then, the Almighty addressed them together saying, go acquire land and find a place to live together. The Almighty commanded them to spend time together. He commanded them to feast together, to celebrate together. He commanded them to record and observe His command of worship and offering. The Almighty commanded the man to govern and be industrious. When the Almighty finished speaking His command, for the nakedness of the man and woman, the Almighty taught them how to make clothing from animal hides so they could fully clothed themselves. He showed the man how to make a weapon. Together, the man and the woman put on their garments. The Almighty had divorced them and sent them away. He told them to beware. He commanded the man and the woman to guard, observe, and maintain His way. The Almighty told them to go stretch themselves out and grow long like the branches of a tree. The man and the woman felt like slaves in bondage who worship the Almighty, the All Supreme Ruler of all the Earth.

The Almighty spoke to His Holy Assembly saying, that Adversary became one flesh with the woman and cause her to read the book of knowledge and perception of good and evil. The Man also became one flesh with the woman and she caused him to read the book of knowledge and perception of good and evil. The Eloheem will say the man is become one of them. Now, the man has experience with wickedness and rebellion, but the man knows how to consider and advise himself. He can discern evil things and bad persons. His experiences with I, the Almighty have been revealed to him, now, he understands and he respects his experiences with the Almighty. He respects the punishment that comes from the Almighty. Now, he is a man of skill. He can comprehend and declare knowledge of the Almighty. He will teach his kinsman good morals and good ethics. He will teach his kinsman to be men of skill. The man will become industrious. He will grow to be prosperous. Because of his conduct, I have dismissed the man from My Holy Land. I have sent him and the woman away. The Adversary, who was alone in his wretchedness, implemented the wicked thoughts of his heart. He has committed the worst act. He has performed the worst deed. He has brought calamity, distress, pain, terror, unhappiness, adversity, grief, harm, and heavy misery upon the species of man. At the vanishing point of this age, I the Almighty, the All Supreme Being, the All Supreme Ruler, the Creator of all things will kill the soul of the Adversary once for all. I will kill and burn up all hypocrites and all those that are in evil in behavior once and for all. Now, by the Book of knowledge, the Book of Life has been revealed to the Adversary. The Book of Life will save a person from sickness, from discouragement, from faintness, and from death. It will preserve a person alive without end, life everlasting along with everlasting prosperity. The world would always be as the beginning generations of humans beings of the world. If he reads the Book of Life, he will always even forevermore be able to devour all flesh on the Earth. His evil destruction and wicked deeds will have an unending future. What if the Adversary reveals this knowledge? What if he stretches out his hand from abroad the coast to any direction to fellowship with the hand of mankind? What if he stretches out his power abroad the coast using force and oppression? What if he stretches out his power abroad the coast to any direction and offers a bounty? What if he stretches out his authority from abroad the coast to any direction using his hand as a creditor or debtor? All of them will choose to accept his offer. All of them will swear to him and use the sword to kill men and beast. All of them will take an oath to him, and use fire to burn up the trees. All of them will vow to him just to lay hold and take possession of the Book of Life. As lightning flashed about the in the land, the Almighty drove the Adversary out of the garden. Created from a time before human beings, the Almighty commanded His Cherubim (**Care-oob**) to dwell among the trees of the garden. Cherubim are mighty spiritual beings under the command of the Almighty. The Almighty commanded His Cherubs to guard the entrance to the garden. Hidden secretly in the thick feathers of their wings, they have a flaming sword that extends along sword's edge and goes to the end point. Their sword is of energy and can transform to and from to be a sword, a knife, a dagger, an axe, or any cutting instrument that has a destructive effect. This is to expel and overthrow the enemy. The sword turns about anyway and on anyone wicked or perverted.

The Almighty commanded Cherubs to wait until the end of the age for HIS command. Then, the Almighty caused thorns to grow thickly around the Book of Life. Now, there was a very narrow view of the Book. The Almighty commanded the Cherubs to stay within the bounds of the book. The Almighty commanded His Cherubs to restrain and expel the Adversary if he returns. The Almighty commanded His Cherubs to protect the Book of Life and wait for His command. The Almighty, in great anger, being greatly displeased, judged the Adversary. He judged the man along with the woman. Being displeased, the Almighty sent them away from His Holy Land. In spite of their rebellion, the Almighty told the Adversary, the man, and the woman that He will requite, indeed, the Almighty promised to fix and avenge the wrongdoing of the Adversary and, altogether, correct the effects of their sin. As the Almighty commanded him, the man observed the night and day. He put a twenty-four-hour period in order and instituted a full working day. From sunrise to sunset, or from one sunset to the next, mankind will use this time to perform labor, be busy, journey, and work to advance and be industrious. After a short time, the woman gave birth to a boy. She called his name Cain (**Kah-yin**). Right after, she gave birth to her second son Cain's brother and she named him Abel (**Hav-vel**). After their births, the woman chose and invited guests to preach to them about the Almighty. She told them the name of her firstborn was Cain (**Kah-yin**). She spoke to them about Cain saying, I have gotten a possession from the creature, but with the help of the Almighty, I have acquired a good man. She spoke to them about Abel (**Hav-vel**) saying, with Abel, the Almighty has restored my soul. The Almighty has revived my life. Abel began keeping sheep and grew to be a shepherd of the people. He cared for them and was a special friend to them. Cain transgressed against the Almighty and made himself to be a husband of the Earth. He worshipped the Earth and enticed others to do the same. He caused people to labor for him and serve as subjects to him. Over the process of time, as an offering to honor the Almighty from a fruit tree, Cain brought a bough ornamented with leaves in front of the altar. Abel brought the firstborn of his flock of sheep in front of the altar. The Almighty had respect for Abel. The Almighty respected his offering, but the Almighty had no respect for Cain nor for his offering. Cain became very and angry and was full of wrath. His desire to do good toward the Almighty fell. The Almighty asked Cain, why are you raging with anger within yourself? Why has your desire to do good toward Me fallen? Sin is sitting and resting at the door of your house. Your desire to sin is like a wild beast craving to devour its prey. Your desire to sin is like a woman longing for a man. Your desire has the power to make you sin. If you desire to sin, then it will direct your life and rule over you. If you do well, I will accept your offering and bless you, but you are not doing well and you will not do well if you indulge in secret hatred. Afterwards, Cain was talking with his brother Abel. As they were speaking to one another, Cain decided to challenge the command that comes from the Almighty. Together, Cain and Abel were in a field. Acting proudly Cain was talking with Abel. Then, Cain stood up against Abel. With his strength, with deadly intent, Cain came against Abel. Cain killed Abel. Cain murdered his brother Abel. By his own hands, Cain put Abel to death. Cain became a murderer.

Afterwards, the Almighty came to Cain and asked, what way is Abel? Where is your brother Abel? Cain answered saying, I have not considered. He has not showed himself. I do not know where he is. I do not care where he is, so I cannot advise You. Am I to treasure him in my memory? Am I to wait for him and watch over him? Am I to guard and preserve him? Am I my brother's keeper? The Almighty responded saying, I hear your brother's voice from the Earth. I hear the sound of your brother's voice as his blood is being shed. I hear the sound of his blood dropping to the ground. His cry for help cries to Me. By the strength and power of your hands, a gaping hole has been torn into the ground. This gaping hole in the Earth has received your brother's body and blood. You covered over the gaping hole that received your brother's body and blood. Now, you will be greatly loathed in the land. I have laid you under a bitter curse and you will be made to be a bitter curse throughout the whole Earth. Now, when you labor upon the ground, its increase will change. When you labor upon the ground, it will not give you its strength, nor its wealth. Afterwards, if you try a second time to labor upon the ground, it will not give you an excess. If you cause someone to be your bondman or your servant and you cause them to labor upon the ground, the ground will not produce an increase for you. Afterwards, if you cause them to try a second time to labor upon the ground, the ground will not be permitted to provide you with more than enough. You will be a fugitive moving to and from upon the whole Earth. You will aimlessly wander backward and forward like a staggering drunkard. You will be disturbed and unstable upon the whole Earth. You will be a vagabond because

I, the Almighty, will cause you to wander. Through the territories and countries, to the ends of the earth, I will cause you to be tossed about the inhabitants that are in the land of the living. The people will judge you as a fugitive and you will tremble like leaves shaking from the wind. They will taunt you with no pity. You will disappear and become a drifter upon the Earth. Cain replied to the Almighty saying, this day, You have driven me away from my family's land. This day, You have divorced me and put me away. This day, You have cast me away from my possession. This day, You have expelled me from the honor of Your presence. Now, You will secretly hide Your purpose for me from me. Therefore, I will hide myself from Your anger. I will hide myself away from Your purpose. I will hide myself away from Your sight. I will be an unstable fugitive wandering to and from upon the Earth. I will wonder aimlessly. Through the territories and countries, to the ends of the Earth, I will be tossed about the inhabitants in the land of the living. I will be pitiful and moan within myself. Therefore, it will come true. Everyone I encounter will detect me. Everyone I encounter will have learned about me. Those that seek me out will kill me with their hands. They will look for me to put me to death. They will murder me. They will make a slaughter of me. I feel the guilt of my sin. I see the perversity of my sin. I understand the depravity of my sin. I understand the consequences of my sin. The punishment for my sin is greatly distinguished by You and, it is of the greatest importance to You. My punishment is very sore and of the greatest intensity. Therefore, I declare my punishment is greater than I can carry. My punishment is greater than I can endure. My punishment is greater than I can contain. I cannot respect the punishment You have given me. I cannot accept the punishment You have given me.

The ALMIGHTY responded saying, whoever kills you Cain will suffer complete vengeance. As their punishment, complete vengeance will be taken in blood. Then, of a miracle, the Almighty caused a distinguishing mark to come upon Cain. To be remembered, as proof of HIS warning, the Almighty fixed that marked to remain upon Cain unless someone fails to know about, except someone fails to see it and makes a slaughter of him. Cain departed away from the presence of the voice of the Almighty. Cain wandered aimlessly as a vagabond. To the east, he wandered to the end of the Earth. He found a land of wilderness. It was a land inhabited by wanderers and those who were exiled. Cain inhabited the land of Nod (**Nohd**). This was a home to those with no land of their own. Cain found a female to be his wife. She was of animal transformation and resembled a woman by appearance. She was a great mistress. As He had sexual affections with her, Cain built a guarded city of excitement, terror, and anguish. Cain's wife became pregnant with a child. At the time of delivery, in distress, she labored and brought forth a child. Of wicked behavior, Cain invited and chose people to preach to. He preached the reputation of the city to them. He preached the honor of the city to them. He brought his new born son before his guests and all those whom he invited. According to his honor, reputation, glory, and authority, Cain named his son Enoch (**Han-noch**). Before all his guests, Cain proclaimed his son's lineage and named the city after his son. And onto Enoch was born Irad (**Ee-rad**). Irad fathered Mehujael (**Mekh-hu-ya-el**). Mehujael fathered Methusael (**meth-thu-sha-el**). Methusael fathered Lamech (**lay-mehk**). Lamech had taken possession of two women to be his wives.

They were females of animal transformation and both resembled a woman by appearance. His first wife was named Adah. His second wife is named Zillah. Adah gave birth to Jabal (**Ya-vaul**). Jabal was respected and honored as the originator of selling livestock. He sold cows, sheep, and goats in herds for personal possession to those that settled down in tents. He sold livestock to those who remained living in tents in the wilderness. His brother's name was Jubal (**Yu-vaul**). He was respected and honored as the originator of those that could manipulate musical instruments. He was one of those that could take a musical instrument like a flute or a reed pipe and skillfully overlay its sound with another musical instrument like a harp or an organ. But he was one of those who defiled music. Zillah gave birth to Tubal-Cain (**Tu-val- ca-in**). He was a hammerer. He hammered out swords and sharpened the edges of them. He was a craftsman of every sharp edged tool made of metal. His lust was in idolatry. He idols of brass, bronze, copper, and iron. He was dubious and he could not be trusted. He made weapons of iron and used the strength of those weapons to oppress. The sister of Tubal Cain was Naamah (**Nah– ah-ma**). Lamech spoke to his wives Adah and Zillah, saying, you wives of Lamech listen to me and pay attention to what I have to say. Listen to me because I have killed a man. I have ruined a man's life. I have murdered a man to my own ruin. I have killed a son of apostasy. He is of a black and blue mark with a mark of stripes on his skin itself. This is to my own death. If Cain is to be avenged completely, then truly for me Lamech, the powerful vengeance will be taken completely on the person that ruins my life. Now, during this time, the first man of mankind went into his wife again with sexual affections. She conceived and gave birth to a son.

he chose and invited guests to preach to. She spoke to them about the Almighty and declared the lineage of her son. She brought her son before them and she spoke to her guests saying, the Almighty has considered me and appointed me a child of good moral quality. In place of my child Abel, whom my firstborn son Cain murdered, the Almighty has appointed certain descendants of this child to be for HIS own righteousness and of this same seed of descendants, the Almighty has appointed a practitioner of His own righteousness. She called the name of her son Seth (**Sheth**). Now, the first man of mankind had a life. He got sick, nourished himself, and was restored to health. He got discouraged, he rested, and he was revived. He became weary, he rested, and he was refreshed. He sustained himself and lived prosperously. He lived one hundred thirty years then fathered a son of his own manners. This son resembled the image of the first man of mankind. The first man of mankind chose and invited guests to preach to. He preached about the Almighty to them, he declared the lineage of his son to them, and called his son's name Seth. After he fathered Seth, the first man of mankind fathered more sons and daughters up until he was eight hundred years old. The first man of mankind lived a total of nine hundred thirty years. As a penalty of neglecting wise conduct and good morals, he died prematurely. Suddenly, he was put to death by a warlock magician of necromancy. Seth fathered a son when he was one hundred five years old. Seth chose and invited guests to preach to. He preached about the Almighty to them, he declared the lineage of his son to them and called his son's name Enos (**ee-ohsh**). Then men began to dishonor the Covenant that comes from the Almighty. They began to treat the Almighty's Covenant as a common thing like it was no better than any other, therefore, men began to pollute themselves and violate the honor of the Almighty. Men began to play defiled music and create defiled plays. Men had begun to profane the authority and the reputation of the Almighty. Men made the honor and glory of the Almighty to be a common thing. Men began to pierce, wound, and kill themselves. Men began to sexually prostitute themselves and men began religious sexual rituals. Men began to proclaim themselves as chosen to preach the name, the honor, the reputation, the glory, and the authority of the Eloheem. They began to name themselves by the names of the Eloheem. They summon themselves with music and begin to read aloud the authority and reputation of the Eloheem. They chose to appoint honor and glory to the reputation of the Eloheem to be a memorial and a monument. After he fathered Enos, Seth fathered more sons and daughters until he was eight hundred seven years old. Seth lived a total of nine hundred twelve years. As a penalty for neglecting wise conduct and good morals, Seth died prematurely. Suddenly, he was put to death by a warlock magician of necromancy. Seth's son Enos (**ee-ohsh**) lived for ninety years, then he fathered Cainan (**Kay-non**). After he fathered Cainan, Enos had more sons and daughters until he was eight hundred fifteen years old. Enos lived for a total nine hundred five years. As a penalty for neglecting wise conduct and good morals, he died prematurely. He was put to death by a warlock magician of necromancy. Cainan lived for seventy years, then he fathered Mahalaleel (**ma-hal-al- ale**). After he fathered Mahalaleel, Cainan fathered more sons and daughters until he was eight hundred forty years old. He lived a total of nine hundred ten years. As a penalty for neglecting wise conduct and good morals, he died prematurely.

Suddenly, he was put to death by a warlock magician of necromancy. Cainan's son Mahalaleel lived sixty-five years, then he fathered Jared (**Yeh-red**). Mahalaleel lived a total eight hundred ninety-five years. As a penalty for neglecting wise conduct and good morals, suddenly, he was put to death by a warlock magician of necromancy. Mahalaleel's son Jared lived for one hundred sixty-two years, then he fathered Hanoch (**khan-oke**). After he fathered Hanoch, Jared had more sons and daughters. Jared lived a total of nine hundred sixty-two years. As a penalty for neglecting wise conduct and good morals, he died prematurely. Suddenly, he was put to death. He was killed by a warlock magician of necromancy. Hanoch lived sixty-five years, then he fathered Methuselah (**meth-thu-shal-lye**). Hanoch grew to be great with the Almighty. He lived according to the Almighty. He walked about and he wandered to and from different places talking with the Almighty and talking to others about the Almighty. He did not die, but he was taken out of the land of the living. The Almighty chose him and accepted him, then carried him away to be His own possession. As lightning flashed about, Hanoch departed away with a whirl wind from the Almighty. Hanoch's son Methuselah lived for one hundred eighty-seven years, then he fathered Lamech (**leh-meh**). After he fathered Lamech, Methuselah fathered more sons and daughters until he was seven hundred eighty-two years old. Methuselah lived a total of nine hundred sixty-nine years. As a penalty for neglecting wise conduct and good morals, Methuselah died prematurely. Suddenly, he was put to death. He was killed by a warlock magician of necromancy. Lamech lived eighty-two years and fathered a son of the Almighty's righteousness. Lamech chose and invited guests to preach to. He preached about the Almighty, he declared his son's lineage, and he called his son's name Noah (**No-akh**). He spoke to his guests saying, this child of mine will sigh deeply and repent to the Almighty to comfort himself. This child of mine will comfort us concerning our work that comes from the Almighty. This child of mine is our comfort concerning our pain, strength, and hardship that we have put forth to accomplish the work that comes from the Almighty. He is our comfort because the whole ground of the Earth and its rulers have been made to be a bitter curse of the Almighty. This child of mine will suffer grief and pity himself yet he will have compassion. He will comfort himself in the work that comes from the Almighty. For an act of judgment that comes from the Almighty, this child of mine will labor to make a product of deliverance. He will accomplish the work that comes from the Almighty. This child of mine will receive the mercy and grace that comes from the ALMIGHTY. After he fathered Noah, Lamech fathered more sons and daughters until he was five hundred ninety-five years old. Lamech lived a total of seven hundred seventy-seven years. As a penalty for neglecting wise conduct and good morals, he died prematurely. Suddenly, he was put to death. He was killed by a warlock magician of necromancy. The species of mankind began to multiply and become many, they began to multiply and become numerous and when the species of mankind became exceedingly great in number upon the Earth, the daughters of men began to be of wicked behavior. The daughters of men brought forth iniquity with the sons of Eloheem. The sons of Eloheem are the sons of injustice. They believed they were of the constellation of Orion. They accepted themselves as fugitives who were judged by the Almighty.

They believed they were of those who were of old that had lost their inheritance. They believed they were of those who were of ancient time who were overwhelmed, overthrown, cast down as inferior and killed out. Because the sons of Eloheem are rebellious against the Almighty, the daughters of men gave their attention to them. Because the sons of Eloheem are rebellious against the Almighty, the daughters of men observed them and desired to learn about them. Because the sons of Eloheem are rebellious against the Almighty, the daughters of men became more appropriate toward them. Because the daughters of men were becoming more appropriate toward them, the daughters of men looked beautiful to sons of Eloheem. The daughters of men looked precious to the sons of Eloheem. When the sons of the Eloheem saw that the daughters of men were cheerful and in favor of them when the sons of Eloheem saw that even the best of the daughters of men were very kind to them and ready to pleasure them, when the sons of Eloheem saw that they could be prosperous with the daughters of men, on these conditions, to the sons of Eloheem, the daughters of men were the apple of the eye. So, the sons of Eloheem appeared and presented themselves onto the daughters of men. The sons of Eloheem took possession of women to be wives for themselves of whomever they wanted. The Almighty summoned and spoke to His Holy Assembly, saying, now, mankind has gone astray again. They are committing an error in their minds. They are committing sin ignorantly with their flesh. Indeed, mankind is deceived again. Mankind is deceived of his body. Mankind is deceived of his organ of generation. Mankind is deceived about his blood relations. Mankind is deceived and confused in knowing whether he is of humans of man or of animals. MY SPIRIT will not quarrel and be at strife with mankind throughout eternity, but until the end of the age, at the vanishing point. My SPIRIT will not always plead with mankind, nor will My SPIRIT always judge and execute judgment against mankind, but until the end of the age, at the vanishing point. Therefore, until the end of the whole age, until the day of trouble and troubled weather, a person's lifetime will be one hundred twenty years or a fraction of it. In those days, as at older times, there were giants and tyrants on the Earth. The daughters of men gained a good understanding of the intelligence of the sons of Eloheem. The daughters of men gained a good understanding of the morals of the sons of Eloheem and how the sons of Eloheem are able prosper. In those days, there were giant bullies on the earth, in the fields, in the countries, in the nations of the world. The daughters of men gained a good understanding of the sexual nature of the sons of Eloheem. The daughters of men came to be of wicked behavior. They gave birth to children for the sons of Eloheem. Those children that were of their same pedigree became giants, mighty men, strong warriors, brave leaders, and powerful tyrants, as at the beginning generations of persons in the world whose people continued in existence to their vanishing point. Their men were mortal persons of mankind. They were more dignified in their pride and blood-thirsty. They were men of individual reputation, men of individual authority, men of individual character, men of individual honor. They were men of fame and glory. For a memorial and a monument, they were of a name designated by their Eloheem. The Almighty looked at the evil of mankind. He gave attention to it and considered. He distinguished the natural, the ethical, and the moral evils that were coming forth of mankind. He observed all their thoughts and actions, and beheld all the worst of mankind.

He advised Himself that the wickedness of mankind was very great and abounding in multitude. He saw that the evilness of mankind greatly injured the land and water. Their wickedness was vicious upon the fields, upon the wilderness, upon the earth, and its inhabitants. It had become a common way for the nations of the world. The Almighty looked upon the misery, distress, pain, sadness, adversity, and unhappiness. He observed that every imagination about how man formed from the soil was altogether for evil. As the Almighty had foreseen, He appeared and caused Himself to be visible before them. The Almighty presented Himself in the sight of others. He wanted them to look at one another's face and consider. He wanted them to give attention to Him, learn about Him, and have experience with Him. The Almighty desired them to distinguish Him, but the Almighty saw that every graven image invented, and every imagination of an All Supreme Being or Creator of all things from the thoughts of mankind was for evil. The Almighty looked at every intellectual device and machine of purpose and saw it was for evil. He looked at and considered all knowledge and understanding of their heart and mind and saw it was for evil. The Almighty saw that mankind's desire to do wickedness was day after day, from sunrise to sunset, from sunset to sunrise continually. Because of this, the Almighty, the Creator of all things sighed from disappointment and lamented from grief. The Almighty Himself suffered the torture of grief for having compassion. To His feelings, it hurt the Almighty to see His command of worship copied and stretched out for evil. It angered the Almighty to see His own character, reputation, honor, and His Word copied and fashioned for evil. Therefore, the Almighty, in the seat of His emotions was not at ease within Himself. The Almighty summoned and spoke to His Holy Assembly saying, I am going to avenge Myself by destroying all of mankind. It is not because I regret creating human persons. It is not because I regret creating mankind, but to comfort Myself, I am sending MY vengeance against all those that have blasphemy My reputation. To comfort Myself, I am sending MY vengeance against all those that have slandered My Honor. To comfort Myself, I am sending MY vengeance against all those whose mind and heart is for evil. I will wipe away all men, all Behemoth, all beast, all cattle, all creatures, all creeping things and all birds of the air. I will wipe them away from the surface of the Earth. Not because I regret creating them, but because they have no compassion toward Me, the Almighty, the All Supreme Being, the All Supreme Ruler, the Creator of all things and because they cause Me to suffer the torture of grief and disappointment. As in former times, at the beginning generations of human persons, from the presence of the Eloheem, the land of the living was spoiled and had gone into ruin. With faces of animals and with faces of persons, these gods, goddesses, angels, rulers, judges, and mighty ones battered and wasted the soil, the fields, and the wildernesses to the ends of the Earth. The nations of the world dealt corruptly and was filled with injustice. The land of the living was overflowing with cruel oppressors. The way of the world was perverse, and the common inhabitants of the world had become morally corrupt. Because of their corruption, the common inhabitants of the Earth satisfied themselves with falsehood, unjust gain, violent dealing, and all unrighteousness. Like He had foreseen, The Almighty considered all the persons of the Earth. He watched them and discerned. The Almighty looked at one person, then at another, then at another, and so on, to distinguish them, to see if He could enjoy them and respect them.

As He was watching, the Almighty saw that all persons of the Earth were perverted and morally corrupt. All persons of the Earth were corrupting the manner of living He appointed to mankind. All persons of the Earth were ruining the moral character He appointed to mankind. All persons of the Earth were corrupting His way of judgment appointed to mankind. But Noah, son of Lamech, found sufficient favor in the sight of the Almighty. In affliction, Noah sought to secure what was lost of the Almighty. Noah sought to find the conditions of thinking that is of the Almighty. Noah sought to learn how to recognize the beauty and preciousness of spirituality that is of the Almighty. Noah sought to learn how to present an offering to the Almighty. Noah sought after the Almighty, the All Supreme Being, the All Supreme Ruler, the Creator of all things. Noah's desire was to be accepted and delivered by the Almighty. Noah walked away from the Eloheem. He did not join those gods, goddesses, angels, and godlike ones. He speedily departed away from their beliefs and behaviors to live his life according to the manner the Almighty appointed to mankind. Proving to be humble and upright, Noah was accepted by the Almighty. Noah was given the kindness and grace that comes from the Almighty because Noah was lawfully correct in the sight of the Almighty. Now, these are the generations of Noah. Noah was a just man and upright in his cause. He governed his life in a just manner. Because he was righteous in conduct and character, the Almighty vindicated and justified him. Having sincerity and integrity, Noah was in accord with the truth of the Almighty, therefore, in the sight of the Almighty he was innocent, perfect, and morally without a blemish in his generations. The Almighty visited Noah and in a dream He spoke to Noah about the Eloheem. The Almighty spoke to Noah saying, the Eloheem thinks, desires, and intend to challenge My command. They boast in themselves and act very proud. They openly use their speech against My authority, My character, My honor, My glory, My reputation, and My report. The Almighty continued speaking to Noah saying, as in former times, by the process of time, the end of this time and space is before Me. Mankind has become morally corrupt. They also think, desire, and intend to challenge My command. They boast in themselves and act very proud. They openly use their speech against My authority, My character, My honor, My glory, My reputation, and My report. All persons of the Earth are corrupting My way of judgment. In its total number, I see the end of all living things. Through the Eloheem, the persons of the Earth have become very violent, and the world is overflowing with injustice. The Earth is filled with cruelty. The Earth is filled with oppressors. The Earth is filled with false witnesses and unjust gain. Now, the persons on the Earth have become accomplished in unrighteousness, and they are satisfied by violence. Look into this vision and see then consider. Look and Behold. I, the Almighty, will bring a flowing deluge of water upon the whole Earth. I, the Almighty, will bring a flood of flowing water upon the land of the living onto all persons of the world. In the land of the living, to the ends of the Earth. I, the ALMIGHTY will bring a flood of danger and violence against all persons of the world. Everything on the Earth, in its totality, will perish. Each living thing and every living being with a soul will breathe out their last breath, their soul will leave their body and they will die.

I, the Almighty will cause all them to perish. To the ends of the Earth, I will destroy all them in the land of the living. Their oppression and violence is at its end. Their cruelty and injustice is at its end. Their false witnessing and unjust gain is at its end. All their unrighteousness is at its end and set to expire. I have accepted you. You cannot be bribed for a life, and the sum of money does not satisfy you. I, the Almighty have established My Covenant and My Ordinance with you. Through you, My Covenant and My Ordinance will endure. Therefore, I have ordained you to keep My Covenant. With you, My alliance with mankind, My friendship with mankind, and My Oath to mankind is fulfilled. You will protect My Covenant and confirm it between men. Do not fear, I will strengthen you and help you. The Almighty continued speaking, saying, Noah, every living thing that is on the earth will die except anything that is with you. Families outside those belonging to your household such as leaders, judges, scribes, and common people of temples, palaces, prisons, and places abroad are outside of reconciliation. They are without ransom and without pardon. You will make an offering to atone for the sin of your household. Then you will build a wooden ship. You attend to it as your own property. You will pardon those that belong to your household, and use the ship to house them. You will enter into the ship and go within it, you, your sons, your wife, and your sons' wives can come in with you. You will build the ship from timber. Within the ship, you will make chambers, rooms, and nests for dwelling. Make the nests be together according to the relationship of the birds and animals. Make the chambers be together according to the relationship of the animals. Make the rooms be together according to the relationship of the beasts and cattle. Make rooms to be together according to the relationship of the Behemoth. You will pitch the ship within the inside so the front and back will move up and down. The length of the ship will be three hundred cubits, the width of it fifty cubits, and the height of it thirty cubits. These are the measurements that you will make it. You will set the door of the wooden vessel on the side thereof. You will make a window and a double light in the ship that starts from the foundation. You will finish it at the top. You will build the ship with a lower floor, a second floor and a third floor. You will be a village covered in a ship. For every kind of living thing, you will allow one male and one female to enter the ship. To kept them alive, you will allow one male and one female as a pair, of every species of unclean animal and unclean living things, you will allow one male and one female that are paired together to enter the ship. From the Behemoth and from every clean beast, from every clean animal, one male and one female as a pair, you will take seven pairs of them into your possession. This is to keep their seed alive on the surface of the Earth. The Almighty continued speaking to Noah saying, by My divine power to see, I foresee by visions and before the first generation of man began, I foresaw your generation and I saw you. I considered you. I observed you present yourself as lawful, righteous in character and conduct according to righteousness that pleases Me. I also foresee the generations of your posterity and in that last generation of your posterity I see a righteous man. I have considered and observed him. I have seen him present himself as lawful, just, righteous in character and conduct according to righteousness that pleases Me. By condition and quality, I have distinguished him among the class of men.

Therefore, I, the Almighty will, in that time period of the age, watch over him and help him. I will justify and vindicate him. In his generation, He will appear before Me to meet Me. Now, in your generation, I have distinguished you among the class of men by condition and quality. I have looked after you and helped you because you are lawful and righteous in My sight. Therefore, you are justified and vindicated by Me, the Almighty. In seven days, I will cause it to pour down rain onto the Earth. Rain will pour down for forty days and for forty nights. Every living thing on dry land with nostrils to breathe air for life that is not in the ship I have commanded you to build will be destroyed and wiped away from the surface of the Earth. You and all those belonging to your household will come into the ship. Noah was five hundred years old when he fathered his sons Shem (**Shame**), Ham (**Kham**), and Japeth (**Yef-feth**). Noah was six hundred years old when the Almighty sent the great flood of water onto the Earth. Noah did as the Almighty commanded and gathered all the living things that the Almighty authorized to go into the ship. Noah had gathered all the food needed for the journey. Then, a mighty wind came forth upon the Earth and brought heavy rain. As the down pouring rain became heavy, Noah went into the ship with his wife, with his sons, and with his sons' wives. Then, the Almighty shut in the door and they were shut in the ship. In the six hundredth year, in the second month, on the seventeenth day of the month of Noah's life, this same day, the clouds of the sky were opened, then all the waters from the great deep sea began to burst through their boundaries. The flood of water increased each day and raised the ship up from the surface of the Earth. The rain continued to pour down onto the earth. The water continued and became exceedingly strong on the earth, then all the high hills that were under the skyline were covered. The flood of water spread over the whole Earth and was fifteen cubits high, then to twenty and one half cubits upward from the surface of the earth. The water continued to increase on the earth, then all the high hills that were under the skyline were covered, and the water continued to increase until the top of the mountains were covered. The ship travel on the surface of the waters and was very high above the surface of the Earth. All flesh that moved on the earth died. Every human, every man, every woman, every child, all the species of Behemoth, all cattle, all beast, all fowl, and every creeping thing that creeps on the earth, all them on dry land whose nostrils took in air for life died. Noah and they that were with him in the ship were the only survivors. It rained onto the earth for forty days and for forty nights. The flood of water was mighty and continued on the earth for one hundred fifty days. The Almighty recorded what He mentioned to Noah to make a remembrance. He had good thoughts on this record and marked it to be recognized, to remind Himself to keep remembrance in His mind. The Almighty was very sincere and very serious about remembering Noah. Therefore, the Almighty remembered Noah, the son of Lamech, and He remembered every living thing, the species of Behemoth, and, all the cattle that was in the ship with Noah. The Almighty, who has the charge of the whole Earth, made His SPIRIT, that is animated of energy, that is as gas, that is like a breath in the cold air, travel over the whole earth and move against the flood of water, then the flood of water began to decrease. The deep seas were restrained. The clouds that move in the sky were shut up. The waters began to return from off the Earth.

The ship settled down and remained calm in the seventh month, on the seventeenth day of the month, on the mountain of Ararat (**Air-rah-rot**). The waters decreased continually, and now, it was the tenth month. In the tenth month, on the first day of the month, the tops of mountains were seen. At the end of forty days, Noah opened the window of the ship and he sent out a female pigeon from the window of the ship but the female pigeon came back to the window. The pigeon found no rest for the soles of her feet. She returned to him inside the ship and the waters were still on the surface of the whole earth. Noah put out his hand and gently grabbed the pigeon and pulled her inside the ship to him. Noah remained another seven days in the ship then he sent out the female pigeon from the window of the ship. The pigeon came back to him in the evening and he saw there was an olive leaf plucked from off a branch in her mouth. Now, Noah knew that the waters were diminishing from off the earth. He remained inside the ship another seven days then sent the female pigeon out of the window but this time she did not return to him anymore. After the end of the one hundred fifty days, the waters covered the earth no more. The Almighty talked to Noah and commanded him saying, you and your wife, your sons and their wives go forth from out of the ship, and bring every living thing, the fowl, the species of Behemoth, the beast, the cattle, the animals, and every creeping thing that is with you so you all can breed and increase abundantly, so you all can be fruitful, and multiply to become very numerous in number upon the Earth. The Almighty spoke to Himself, within His own mind, as if reminding Himself to be prepared saying by their imaginations, the mind in human beings is evil from the time of their youth. By their thoughts, men are evil from the time of their childhood. By their knowledge, human beings are evil from the time of their youth. By their creation of idols, men are evil from the time of their youth. The intelligent devices they use for the purpose of work are used for evil. Then the Almighty delighted to see Noah's burnt offering. It was soothing and pleasant to the Almighty. The Almighty accepted Noah's burnt offering that was as a sweet smell being blown by the wind. The Almighty accepted Noah's sacrifice that was as a sweet aroma being blown by the wind. In His mind, the Almighty spoke to Himself saying, I will not increase the curse that is on the whole earth again. I will not do more to further the curse that is on the whole Earth. I will not lightly esteem the curse that is on the whole Earth to make it more despicable. I will make not make the curse that is on the whole Earth insignificant to increase the dishonor of it. For the sake of a certain Man, and certain persons of His nation who will become a new individual species of mankind, I will not exceed the curse that is on the whole Earth. As I have observed and accomplished, I will not kill every living thing on dry Earth anymore. I will not put an attack in order and appoint it to destroy every living on dry Earth anymore. The soil, the fields, and the wilderness of the Earth will remain forever, therefore, seedtime, the time of sowing seed and its harvest, the time of harvesting crop will not be removed nor will it rest, neither will it be put to an end. The soil, the fields, and the wilderness of the whole Earth will remain forever, therefore, the autumn season when crops are gathered nor the cold of the winter season will be removed. These seasons will not rest nor be put to an end.

The soil, the fields, and the wilderness of the whole Earth will remain forever, therefore, the warm spring nor the hot dry season will be removed. These seasons will not rest nor be put to an end. The soil, the fields, and the wilderness of the whole Earth will remain forever, therefore, the daytime, the working day, the day's journey, and the gloom of night will not be removed. These things will not rest nor be put to an end. The soil, the fields, and the wilderness of the whole Earth will remain forever, therefore, the twenty-four hour period, from sunrise to sunset, from sunset to sunrise, that is the yesterday, the today, and the tomorrow will not be removed. These things will not rest nor be put to an end. The soil, the fields, and the wilderness of the whole Earth will remain forever, therefore, at the end of the whole age, MY practitioner of righteousness and the descendants of moral quality will not fail to come. These certain people will not be removed nor will they be put to an end. The Almighty loved Noah. He blessed Noah and his sons altogether. The Almighty spoke to Noah and commanded him, saying, be fruitful, show fruitfulness, branch off, grow, increase, and bring forth fruit. The Almighty commanded Noah to command all those on his ship to multiply themselves in number and excel. He commanded them to continue multiplying and become many people. He commanded them to multiply and become very numerous in number. He commanded them to multiply and become exceeding great in number. The Almighty commanded them to set themselves apart and become accomplished. He commanded them to satisfy themselves with the abundance of the Earth and replenish the ground, the fields, the wilderness, and the countries with inhabitants. Now, Noah is an object of reverence.

He is an object of terribleness and the fear of him will be upon every beast of the Earth, upon every fowl of the air, upon all that moves upon the Earth, and upon the fishes of the sea. All the things in the world is appointed to be under Noah's dominion. They were assigned to be under his charge. They are delivered into the power and strength of his hands. Of Noah's judgment, he decides what can be eaten of all living things that breathe air to live. The Almighty visited Noah and spoke to him saying, every living thing that has blood in the flesh, that Noah judges to be an object of food will be consumed in fire. I, the Almighty, the All Supreme Being, the All Supreme Ruler have given you all things, but the fleshy body of humans you will not eat. You will not eat blood. You will not feed on drops of blood. You will not be blood thirsty. You will not devour persons with oppression. You will not kill an innocent person. Surely, I, the Almighty, the All Supreme Being, the All Supreme Ruler will search out, investigate, and require the blood of bloodthirsty necromancers and bloodthirsty heathen gods who require worship and shedding blood. Surely, I will search out, investigate, and require the blood of any living being that resorts to the strength of heathen deities or necromancers to shed blood. Certainly, I will search out and investigate the life, the mind, the desire, the appetite, the passions, and the soul of any human being who causes death by their own hand or who is bloodthirsty; or who sheds the blood of the innocent, and I will require their blood. I will search out, investigate, and require the blood of any heathen god and necromancer that demand to be worshipped as any kind of beast. I will search out, investigate, and require the blood of any heathen deity and necromancer that require you to study, practice, and resort to the dominion, the power, and strength of any beast.

I will search out, investigate, and require the blood of any human being or any person of mankind that devours another with oppression. I will search out, investigate, and require the blood of any human being or any person of mankind with dominion, power, or strength and demand themselves to be worshipped as an animal or god. I, the ALMIGHTY, will search out, investigate, and require the blood of any human or any person of mankind that studies, practices, and resorts to any heathen deity or necromancer for ministry, for dominion, for power, for oppression, or for strength. Whether a servant, a mighty man, or a champion, I will require the life of any person that prays, worships, or resorts to heathen deities or necromancers that require the blood of a person or the blood of any living thing. Whether a servant, a mighty man, or a champion, I will demand the life of any person that studies, practices, and follows a heathen deity or necromancer who requires blood. I will demand the life any beast that sheds the blood of a person. Whosoever pours out the anger of their heart and sheds the blood of a person, then by a person pouring out anger from their heart will this person's blood be shed. Man resembles the image of Eloheem, but mankind's ability to work and accomplish, mankind's ability to perform and execute, mankind's ability to prepare and put in order, mankind's ability to observe and attend to, mankind's ability to institute and appoint, mankind's ability to celebrate and act with effect is from the likeness of the Almighty, the All Supreme Being, the Creator of all things. The Almighty continued speaking to Noah saying, I have established My Covenant and My Ordinance you. I have ordained you to establish My Ordinance and confirm My Covenant between men.

With you, I maintain My alliance with mankind. With you, I will maintain My friendship with mankind. With you, I fulfill the Seventh Oath I took to preserve mankind and the Earth. You will investigate any violation of My Covenant because it is fixed upon you and binding upon you to keep. After your time, I will establish My Covenant with children of your semen, and they will maintain My Ordinance and confirm My Covenant between men. After that, I will continue to My Covenant and My Ordinance with your descendants. Following after, at the hinder part of your posterity, I have ordained a practitioner of righteousness of your lineage, and certain descendants of your lineage who are of moral quality to arise stirred up. They will be made to be powerful, and they will come on the scene in hostility toward all those who violate My Covenant. These persons will maintain My Ordinance and establish My Covenant between men. With them, I will maintain My alliance with mankind. With them, I will maintain My friendship with mankind. With them, I will fulfill the Seventh Oath I took to preserve mankind and the Earth. These certain persons will impose My Ordinance and My Covenant upon all mankind to the ends of the Earth. They will carry out and maintain the duties of My Ordinance and My Covenant. They will investigate and judge any violation of My Ordinance and My Covenant because it will be fixed upon them and binding upon them to keep. I will cause them to become established and endure. The purpose of My Ordinance and My Covenant will be fulfilled. Now, My Ordinance and My Covenant are upon all living things. I made MY COVENANT to be between all the living things on the ship.

Noah, because I have established My Covenant with you, because I have established My Law with you, because I have established My alliance with you, I will not eliminate all flesh of mankind from My Covenant nor My Law. The flesh of mankind will not be cut off from My Covenant nor My Law. My Covenant with you and all your descendants will not perish, nor will all flesh be cut off by a flood of raging water. To you, to all your descendants, and to all living things that were on the ship with you, MY Covenant is to be a monument and a memorial. My Covenant is to be always remembered, therefore, for a token of remembrance, I have created a rainbow. I have appointed My rainbow to stretch out among the clouds and the sky. My rainbow is proof and a sign to be remembered. I have recorded My Covenant between Me and you, between Me and all your descendants, between Me and all living things that were on the ship. I will think well upon My Covenant and it will always be remembered in My mind. The Almighty finished speaking to Noah. The sons of Noah departed the ship with their father Noah. Then, they went forth onto the Earth with a purpose. Noah's sons were Shem (**Shame**), Ham, (**Kham**), and Japheth (**Yef-pheth**). These are the three sons of Noah and onto them, all the Earth was in their possession. Noah began his inheritance and stewardship of the Earth. As he stewarded all living things, Noah began to become a great man and a mighty servant, but over the process of time, he began to greatly transgress. Then, people began to break the Covenant and the Law of the Almighty. Men began to wound and kill each other. Men began to dishonor and defile themselves. Men began to prostitute themselves ritually and sexually. They began to make and play defiled music.

Then, these things began to be common and were treated as being common. At this time, the sons of Ham were Cush (**Koosh**), Mizraim (**Mitz-rye-em**), Phut (**phoot**), and Canaan (**ken-ah-an**). The sons of Shem were Elam(**Ay-lam**), Asshur (**Ash-shore**), and Arphaxad(**Air-pak-shad**). Arphaxad was born to Shem two years after the flood, and Shem was one hundred years old. Noah had planted a garden and established a vineyard. He had a banquet with defiled music. Like a winebibber, Noah feasted and drank a lot of intoxicating wine. He was filled abundantly with the drink of wine and he was great in his merriness. He had caused himself to become very intoxicated. Indeed, he was very drunk. He became so drunk, Noah had to be carried inside his tent and those that helped him left him undefended. He was left uncovered to be discovered. As foresaw by the ALMIGHTY, in the sight of others, Canaan (**ken-ah-an**)was brought to see his father's nakedness. Those with him gave him advice. Afterwards, Canaan took heed. He appeared in his father's tent. He uncovered himself and presented himself before his father's nakedness. Canaan observed his father's nakedness and joyfully looked at his father. Canaan looked at Noah's face and gazed upon his nakedness with approval. Of indecency and improper behavior, Canaan enjoyed being near the nakedness of his father. He did not report it to his two brothers. He did not make it known to his brethren. Shem and Japheth took a garment and placed it upon both their shoulders, and walked backwards, then covered the indecency, the nakedness of their father. Their faces were turned away so they could not see the indecency of their father's improper behavior. Noah became active and awoke from his intoxication of wine. Noah considered. He was wise and acquainted with carnally knowing a person.

Then, he discerned and it was revealed onto him. He understood what his grandson had done to him. Noah called for his sons. He spoke to them saying, Canaan has been laid under a bitter curse and he is going to be made to be a bitter curse. Cursed be Canaan, on all sides, he will be a slave of slaves to his brothers and his brethren. For the treason and blasphemies of the Eloheem, a bitter curse is upon them and their god king. Altogether, they will be made to be a bitter curse. Adoration, praise, and blessings be to the works and possessions of Shem and Canaan will be his servant. Japheth is a silly one, simple, naïve, and gullible. The Eloheem will entice him and deceive him. The Eloheem will allure, flatter, and, persuade him to have a very open mind, a very open morality, and a very open mentality. His descendants will establish themselves and stay in Shem's place of habitation. Japheth's descendants will establish their rest in the sacred tabernacle that Shem establishes to honor the Almighty. On all sides, Canaan will be his servant. After the flood, Noah lived three hundred fifty years. All the time of Noah was nine hundred fifty years. As a penalty of neglecting wise conduct and good morals, Noah died prematurely. Suddenly, he was put to death. He was killed by a warlock magician of necromancy. After the flood, these are the descending generations of the sons of Noah. After the flood, sons were born onto Shem, Ham, and Japheth. Shem is the eldest of son Noah. He is the progenitor of the Semitic tribes of people. Shem became a great and noble man. He was distinguished of men in greatness and in the important things of the Almighty. In respect and honor, he is the chief ancestor of all the children of Eber (**Ay-vair**). The children of Eber are of Shem's class of person.

They are of Shem's good nature. As Shem, they are very kind-hearted, very caring, very compassionate, very tolerant, and very charitable. The sons of Shem (**Shame**) are Elam (**Ay-lam**) and Asshur (**Ash-shore**). Asshur is Shem's second son and progenitor of the Assyrian people. Arphaxad (**Air-pak-shad**) is Shem's third son, Lud (**Lewd**) is the fourth son of Shem and the progenitor of the Lydians. Aram (**air-ram**) or (air-rum), is the fifth son of Shem and the progenitor of the Arameans. The children of Aram (**Air-ram**) are Uz (**ootsis thecountry of Job**), Hul (**khool**), Gether (**Geth-their**) (his region was named after him), and Mash (Mash). The third son of Shem (Shame) is Arphaxad (**Air-pak-shad**) and he fathered Salah (**Sheh-lakh**). Salah fathered Eber (**Ay-vair**). Onto Eber (**Ay-vair**) two sons were born. The name of firstborn was Peleg (**Pel-leg**) for in his time, in the days of his lifetime an earthquake broke the earth into pieces so the whole earth was divided. His brother's name is Joktan (**Yoke-tawn**). Joktan (**Yoke-tawn**) fathered Almodad (**Al-mo-dad**), then Sheleph (**Shel-lef**), then Hazarmaveth (**Hatz-air-ma-veth**), then Jerah (**Yeh-rakh**). Then Joktan (**Yoke-tawn**) fathered Hadoram (Had-o-rum), then Uzal (**Oo-zal**), then Diklah (**Dik-lah**), then Obal (**O-val**), then Abimael (**A-vee-ma-ale**), then Sheba (**Sheh-vah**) Then Ophir (**O-pheer**), then Havilah (**Hav-ve-lah**), then, the last in order of the sons of Joktan (**Yoke-tawn**) is Jobab (**Yo-vav**). These were all the sons of Joktan (**Yoke-tawn**). Their places of dwelling, their places of sojourning, their places of sitting in assembly, and their places of habitation was from Mesha (**May-shah**), as you travel onto Sephar (**Seh-far**), a country of mountains and hills in the east. These are the sons of Shem, according to their families, according to their kindred species, according to their aristocrats, according to their class of persons, according to their circle of relatives, after their languages, after tongues, in their lands, according to their nations. Japheth is Noah's youngest son.

The sons of Japheth are Gomer (**Go-mairare the first of Cimmerians**), Magog (**Ma-gogare barbarians**), Madai (**ma-da-eeare first of Medes or Media**), Javan (**Yah-van**) (**first of Ionia or Grecia**), Tubal (**Tu-val**), Meshech (**Meh-shehare barbarians**), and Tiras (**Tee-ras**). The sons of Gomer are Ashkenaz, and Riphath (**Ree-faph**), and Togarmah (**Toe-gair-mah**). The sons of Javan are Elishah (**el-lee-shah**), and Tarshish (**tair-sheesh**), Kittim (**kit-teen**), and Dodanim (**doe-da-neem**). These persons are Gentiles. They are a heathen nation of people. They are as troops of animals or as a swarm of locusts. The island countries of coastal shores were dispersed and divided among them according to their language. In their nations, they divided and dispersed their people into their appointed lands according to aristocrats, according to species, according to class of persons, and according to circle of relatives. Every one of them spoke with a tongue of fire. Everyone one of them was a babbler. Every one of them spoke for evil. Ham is the second son of Noah. The sons of Ham are Cush (Kush are Ethiopians), and Mizraim (**Mitz-Rye-em are Egyptians**), and Phut (**phoot are Libyans**), and Canaan (**ken-ah-an are Canaanites**). The sons of Cush are Seba (**Seh-va**), Havilah (**Chav-ve-lah**), Sabtah (**Sav-tah**), Raamah (**Rah-mah**), and Sabtecha (**Sav-the-hah**), and Nimrod (**Nim-road**). The sons of Raamah are Sheba (**Shev-vah are Sabeans**), and Dedan (**da-dan**). Mizraim (**Mitz-Rye-em**) fathered Ludim (**Lu-dee**), Anamim (**Ana-meem are a tribe of Egyptians**), Lehabim (**leh-ha-veem are a tribe of Egyptians**), Naphtuhim (**Naph-ta-heem are a tribe of Egyptians**), Pathrusim (**Path-ru-seem are the first of Pathros**), Casluhim (**Cas-la-heem are** whom the Philisteens came out of) and Caphtorim (**kaf-tore are the first Cretans**). The sons of Canaan are Sidon (**See-doan**). Sidon was mixed of man and animal. He was a king. The second son of Canaan is Heth (**Haith**). He is the progenitor of the Hittites. The third son of Canaan is Jebus (**Yeh-vu**). He is the progenitor of the Jebusite (**Yeh-vu-see**). The Jebusite lived in or around the site of Jebus. Jebus is an early name for Jerusalem. Canaan was also the progenitor of the Amorite (**Em-ore-ree**), the Girgasite (**Gear-gah-shee**), the Hivite (**Hiv-vee**), the Arkite (**Air-kee are inhabitants of Erek**), the Sinite (**See-nee**), the Arvadite (**Air-vad**), the Zemarite (**Sem-ah-ree**), and the Hamathite (**Ham-moth**). The border of the Canaanites dark territory was from Sidon (**See-doan**) as you come to Gerar (**Gher-rar**) onto Gaza (**Azz-zah**) as you go onto Sodom (**Seh-dome**) to Gomorrah (**Am-o-rah**) to Admah (**Ad-mah**) to Zeboim (**Seh-o-eem**) onto Lasha (**Leh-shai**). After time, the descendants of these families, these class of persons and their kindred species were dashed to pieces and spread abroad. These are the sons, grandsons, and, descending children of Ham (**Kham**). There some of man and of animal. There were some whom were called angels of Eloheem. In the land of the living, in the fields, in the wilderness, in the city-states of the land, to the ends of the whole Earth, these are the people of Ham's nation according to their families and according to their kindred species. These persons are Gentiles. They are a heathen nation of people. They are as troops of animals or a swarm of locusts. In their nations, they divided and dispersed their people into their appointed lands according to aristocrats, according to species, according to class of persons, and according to circle of relatives. Every one of them spoke with a tongue of fire. Everyone one of them was a babbler. Every one of them spoke for evil. These are all the families of the sons of Noah, in their nations, and after their generations. After the flood, by these families, the nations were divided in the earth. Now, Cush fathered Nimrod (**Nim-road**).

After Nimrod came into being, he arose to be a giant in size. He became the strongest warrior and champion in the Earth, then he began to break his word among men. He began ritually and sexually defiling himself. He began to wound and kill persons. He began to dishonor and violate the Covenant and the Law of the Almighty. He treated the honor, the reputation, the authority, the place, and the glory of the Almighty as a common thing. Nimrod started taking the inheritance of men. He established himself as a beacon and continued to remain as a beacon to the people. He became mighty and the first tyrant and warrior king after the flood to be on the ground, in the fields, in the wilderness, in the countries of the whole Earth. He was a giant and the strongest warrior. Like a hunter, Nimrod was a champion of men who excelled in the chase of prey. In the presence of the angels of the Eloheem, he was a mighty king. In the sight of the Almighty, he was a powerful tyrant, and the strongest warrior of those who hunt and lie in wait. Nimrod desired to challenge the command that comes from the Almighty. Of Nimrod's self-boasting, all his power and might was declared and openly published saying, Nimrod, the powerful giant, the strongest warrior and champion of men. Nimrod, the mighty king in the presence of the Eloheem. Nimrod, the mightiest warrior and a powerful champion against the presence of the Almighty, the All Supreme Being, the All Supreme Ruler. By time and rank, the first of his reign of sovereignty, the beginning of Nimrod's kingdom, the first place was Babel (**Bah-bel**) in the land of Shinar of Babylon, then Erech (**Er-rek**) with some saying **(Ur-ruk)**. **(in the Aramaic language Uruk was knownto be called Erech)** After Erech there was Accad (**Akkad**) then Calneh

(**Cal-neh**). Calneh meant fortress of Anu. All these cities were in the land of Shinar of Babylon. Within the time these cities were established, Asshur (**Ash-shore**), the second son of Shem (**Shame**) departed away from the inhabitants, the fields, and the wilderness in the land of Shinar of Babylon. Asshur went forth with a purpose. He obtained children and established a family. Asshur is the progenitor of the Assyrian people. He built and established guarded cities of excitement, guarded cities of terror, and guarded cities of anguish. He built the city of Nineveh (**Nee-nah-veh**), the city of Rehoboth (**Rek-hoe-bothe**), and the city of Calah (**kel-lakh**). Between Nineveh and Calah, he built the city of Resen (**Reh-sen**). Resen was a very proud city that is distinguished among men in its importance to a god of the Eloheem. This city was very loud and great in its intensity. In Resen, the mighty men were great in number. It was in this time of the age that most persons on the Earth were speaking the same language. Most persons on the Earth had a common way of speaking. Most persons on the Earth were united under one language. Most persons on the Earth were speaking about one power and one commandment. Most persons of the Earth were talking and singing about one work, one duty, one purpose, one judgment, and one glory. Most persons of on the Earth were speaking vain words and lying about the affairs of the Almighty. Most persons on Earth were speaking prophetical lies pertaining to the promise that comes from the Almighty. As Nimrod reigned securely over all persons on the Earth, the same lies were being given to most persons on the Earth. All the princes of Nimrod along with his great men took counsel together. They were joined with the families of Phut, the families of Mitzraim, the families of Cush, and the families of Canaan. They spoke one man to another man. They talked one human being to another human being.

They spoke one servant of the Eloheem to another servant of the Eloheem. Altogether, they openly spoke against the commandment that comes from the Almighty. Altogether, acting proudly, in their own self boasting, they considered in their hearts. As they considered, they desired, then they demanded of each other to challenge the command, the authority, the reputation, the honor, and the glory of the Almighty. They spoke to one to another saying, come now, come on to put on glory. Let us build ourselves a city of excitement. Let us establish families in this city. Let it be a pyramidal city with a tower that has an elevated pulpit. Let us build this tower and let its top reach onto the sky where the clouds move. Let its top reach onto stars of heaven where the celestial bodies revolve. Let its tip top reach onto the Heaven of this Almighty, this All Supreme Being, this All Supreme Ruler. Let our king, who is the best of our chiefs, whose head is of man and animal reach onto the Heaven of this Almighty, this All Supreme Ruler. Let our company of chiefs, in their total number, whose heads are of man and animal reach onto the Heaven of this Almighty, this All Supreme Ruler. Now, let us work and accomplish. Let us acquire this All Supreme Ruler's property and put it in the charge of our king who then will ordain, appoint, and institute over all things. Then, let us make offerings, let us feast and celebrate in the work we have accomplished. Let us make ourselves a name and reputation of honor and glory. Let us make ourselves a name of authority for a memorial, unless we be broken into pieces and scattered abroad as the angels of Eloheem before this time were overflowed, shattered to pieces, and dispersed upon the surface of the whole Earth by the presence of this Almighty, this All Supreme

Ruler. Altogether, they openly spoke against the commandment that comes from the Almighty. They demanded of each other to challenge the command, the authority, the reputation, the honor, and the glory of the Almighty. They said, come now, come on to put on glory. Let us make purified bricks by cremation. Let us thoroughly burn our bricks to make them become white. They used brick for stone that they established using bubbling cement and a slime from the slime pits for mortar they made brick. From His own vision, from before the beginning generations of the first man, the Almighty knew about their revelation. He had foreseen their time, so the Almighty, the All Supreme Ruler descended. Now, the Almighty had come down from His own dwelling to consider the city and the tower being directed by the angels of the Eloheem. They are the kindred species to man. A species of human being of animal transformation. Now, the Almighty had come down to distinguish their city and observe the hypocrites that were striving against Him. After considering, the Almighty summoned and spoke to His Holy Assembly saying, these persons of the Eloheem, these kindred of men, and the people of the nations have altogether become one congregated unit. They all talk with vain words and this one language is binding them together. They have begun an evil plot to acquire My possessions and My property. Their desire is to put it in charge of their king who will ordain, appoint, and institute. They are striving to accomplish their work. The Almighty continued speaking saying, I will feed these animals confusion. Like they have mingled themselves among one another, I will mix their language so they will not be able to understand one another's speech. I will confuse how they talk so they will not be able to understand their judges' proclamations. When the Almighty confused their language, they could not understand one another's talk. As they were building the tower suddenly many of them fell a violent death, and all their work came to an end.

As the Almighty caused many of them to fall a violent death, He caused those who were left alive to scatter themselves throughout the fields, throughout the wilderness to the ends of the Earth. The Almighty dashed their work to pieces. The city was left unoccupied. Everything they were building was left undone. Because the Almighty fed those animals confusion and caused their language to fade away because He confounded their vain words, the Almighty chose to call that place Babel (**Bah-bel**) of Babylonia. He chose to call all those persons of Babel, Babylonians. Shem (**Shame**) is Noah's eldest son. Shem was one hundred years old when he fathered Arphaxad (**air-pack-shad**). This was two years after the flood. Arphaxad (**air-pack-shad**) was Shem's third son. After Shem fathered Arphaxad, Shem fathered mores sons and daughters until he was five hundred years old. Arphaxad lived thirty-five years, then he fathered Salah (**Sheh-lakh**). After he fathered Salah, Arphaxad fathered more sons and daughters until he was four hundred three years old. Salah lived thirty years then fathered Eber (**Ay-vair**). After he fathered Eber, Salah fathered more sons and daughters until he was four hundred three years old. Eber lived thirty-four years then fathered Peleg (**Pel-leg**). Peleg lived thirty years then he fathered Reu (**Reh-oo**). After Peleg fathered Reu, Peleg fathered more sons and daughters until was two hundred nine years old. Reu lived thirty-two years then he fathered Serug (**Seh-roog**). After Reu fathered Serug, Reu fathered more sons and daughters until he was two hundred seven years old. Serug lived thirty years then he fathered Nahor (**Nah-hore**). After he fathered Nahor, Serug fathered more sons and daughters until he was two hundred years old. Nahor lived twenty-nine years then he fathered Terah (**Teh-rath**). After he fathered Terah, Nahor fathered more sons and daughters until he was one hundred nineteen years old. These are the generations of Terah. Terah lived seventy years then he fathered Abram (**Av-rum**), Nahor, and Haran (**Hah-run**). Abram (**Av-rum**) and Nahor (**Nah-hore**) chose wives for themselves. The name of Abram's wife was Sarai (**Sar-rhye**). Sarai had the authority, honor, and reputation of a princess. The name of Nahor's wife was Milcah (**Mil-Cah**). Milcah was the adopted-daughter of Haran (**Hah-run**). She had the authority, reputation, and honor of a queen. Haran fathered Lot (**Lote**). Haran was the father of Milcah and he was the father of Iscah (**Yis-cah**). Iscah is the sister of Lot (**Lote**). As a penalty of neglecting wise conduct and good morals, Haran died prematurely. Suddenly, he was put to death. He was killed by a warlock magician of necromancy. He was executed in the land where he was born, in the land of his kindred, in the city-state of Ur (**oo-ore**), a city of moon worship, in Chaldee (**Cas-dee**), of the Chaldean in southern Babylonia. The Chaldee are the seed of Chesed (**keh-sed**). Chesed is the fourth son of Nahor. Nahor is Abram's younger brother. Now, Abram's wife Sarai was barren. Her reproductive organs were sterile, therefore, she had no children. Terah (**Teh-rath**) took his son Abram (Av-rum). He took his daughter in law, Abram's wife, Sarai (**Sar-rhy**), and Terah took his grandson Lot. Lot is the son of Haran. Terah led them away from southern Babylonia, away from the city-state of Ur (**oo-ore**), a city of moon worship, in Chaldee (**Cas-dee**), of the Chaldeans. They went forth into the land of Canaan (Ken-na-an) until they came onto Haran (**Cah-run**), then they dwelt there for a habitation. The lifetime of Terah (**Teh-rath**) is measured at two hundred five years old. As a penalty of neglecting wise conduct and good morals, Terah died prematurely. Suddenly, he was put to death. He was killed by a warlock magician of necromancy.

erah died in Haran (**Cah-run**). In a vision, the Almighty came and visited Abram. The Almighty spoke to him saying, you get out of your country, and away from your kindred. Get away from your father's house and go forth onto the land that I have caused you to see by vision. You go forth onto this land that you have observed and considered. When I caused you to see the land in your vision, you distinguished it. Now, I will lead you and show you where to find it. I will accomplish a very great work of you. You are appointed to acquire the land for your own property. From you, I have ordained certain descendants and I will prepare them to be a nation. They will make offerings and have celebrations to Me. They will observe and attend to the important things of Me. Of their posterity, at the end of their service, those of them who are righteous and praise Me, the Almighty, I will make them to be a greater nation of people. These persons will be much more noble, and greater in importance. They will be greater in number, greater in intensity, more proud, and louder in sound. I will make them distinguished of men and they will be a nation of mighty men. All them will observe, institute, celebrate, and attend to the important things of Me. Now, I will bless you abundantly. I will cause you to be powerful, praised, and adored. Altogether, I will bless them abundantly. I will cause them to be powerful, praised, and adored. I will make your name, your honor, your reputation, and your glory become great. Altogether, I will cause their name, their honor, their reputation, and glory to be great. Like a gift is presented to be a blessing, you will be presented as the praise and blessing of the Almighty. I have established My treaty of peace with you. By My source of blessing, you will be a blessing. By My source of prosperity, you will prosper. Altogether, they also will be presented as the praise and blessing of the Almighty. They will have possession of My treaty of peace. By My source of blessing, they will be a blessing. By MY source of prosperity, they will prosper. I will bless and him that blesses you. I will love him who loves you. I will put him that dishonors you under a bitter curse and he will be made to be a bitter curse. I will put him that treats you as trifling under a bitter curse and he will be made to be a bitter curse. I will put him that treats you with no value under a bitter curse and he will be made to be a bitter curse. Therefore, I will lay him that curses you under a bitter curse and he will be made to be a bitter curse. All class of families, all kindred species, all people of professions, all kindred species of man even all species of the whole Earth will be adored and blessed by praising, adoring, and blessing you. The Almighty had spoken onto him and Abram obeyed. He departed away from Haran (**Cah-run**). Abram was seventy-five years old when he departed away from Haran. Abram took his wife, Sarai, and his brother's son Lot, all their substance that they had gathered, and the property of persons they had acquired in Haran. They went forth to go into the land of Canaan (**Ken-nah-an**). In their total number, they came into the land of Canaan and introduced themselves to the land. Abram crossed through the fields and the wilderness. Abram passed through the land onto the place of Sichem (**Shak-em**), then onto a great tree on the plain of Moreh (**Mor-reh**). Then, Abram saw the Canaanite (**Ken-nah-an-nee**) in fields, and wilderness of the land. As he rested, by vision, the Almighty appeared onto Abram and advised him. The Almighty declared onto Abram saying, I will give this land onto the children of your semen, to your descendants, and your posterity. Abram set up and built an altar there to honor the Almighty who had appeared onto him by vision to advise him.

Abram departed away from there and went onto a mountain east of Luz (**looz**), then having Luz on the west and Hai (**hye**) on the east, he pitched his tent. Abram set up and built an altar to honor the Almighty. Abram invited those guests who were with him to preach to them. He preached aloud the report that came from the Almighty. He proclaimed the honor, the authority, the reputation, and the glory of the Almighty to be for a memorial. Then, Abram departed away and journeyed onward, walking toward the south. Then, there was hunger and famine in the land. Because the famine was massive, very oppressive, and grievous in the land, Abram turned away from the road and went into Egypt (**Mitz-rhy-em**). There, he was a stranger seeking hospitality. There, he was a sojourner seeking to live there for a period of time. It came to pass, when Abram had come near to enter into Egypt (**Mitz-rhy-em**), he spoke onto his wife, and commanded Sarai (**Sar-rhye**), saying, now, I know you are married to me. I know you are an excellent woman. You are a beautiful woman. You are formed goodly, and it is pleasant to look upon your appearance. Women opposite to men, and those of our kindred species see you as pleasant to look upon. The Egyptians (**Mitz-rhy-em**) will consider and watch you. They will gaze at you and desire you. They will want to have experience with you, so they will appear and present themselves to you, and they will be searching for you. Now, when the Egyptians see you with me, they will say, this is his wife, then they will kill me. They will save you to keep you alive for themselves. Promise me you will tell them, you are my sister. I pray you speak like this. Then, it may be well with me for your sake and my soul will live because of you. It came to pass, when Abram had come into Egypt, the Egyptians looked at Abram's wife. They saw she was extremely beautiful. She was a very excellent woman. The prince, the governors, the noble officials, the people of rank and dignity, the angels of the Eloheem for the Pharaoh (**Pair-oh**) saw her. The Pharaoh saw her also. Together, they praised and boasted of her. They commended her before Pharaoh. The Pharaoh (**Pair-oh**) is a god-king and the Egyptian ruler of rulers. Now, Abram's wife was chosen to be taken into the Pharaoh's house and the Pharaoh accepted Abram. The Pharaoh dealt well with Abram. The Pharaoh did what was right. He did good things for Abram. Abram was well for Sarah's sake. Abram had sheep, oxen, he asses, she asses, menservants, maidservants, and camels. Now, the Almighty had cast punishment, disease, and plague onto Pharaoh and his house. With great intensity, the Almighty struck Pharaoh and his house with leprosy and also of other plagues. The noblemen distinguished these plagues to be of the Almighty Himself. The Almighty cast punishment because of the Pharaoh's actions, because of his commandment, because of the things he spoke of concerning Abram's (**Av-ram**) wife, Sarai (**Sar-rhy**). Pharaoh sent for Abram and called Abram before him. Pharaoh spoke to him asking, what is this that you have done onto me? Why did you not tell me that Sarah is your wife? Why did you say she is my sister? I might have taken her to me for a wife. Now, look at your wife. Take her, go your way, and watch over her. Pharaoh commanded his men concerning Abram and they sent him, his wife Sarah, and all that he had away. With his wife Sarah, with lot, and with all that he had, Abram departed out of Egypt and went back into the south of Canaan. Now, Abram was very rich in cattle, in silver, and in gold. In the south, he journeyed to Luz (**looz**), from there, he went onto the place where his tent had been at the beginning, between Luz and Hai (**hye**). Abram journeyed back onto the place of the altar he built.

The Canaanite (**Ken-nat-ah-nee**) and the Perizzite (**Per-rah-zee**) dwell in the open country of the land. There, Abram invited those guests who were with him and preached to them. He preached the report and the Almighty's proclamation aloud. He proclaimed the honor, the authority, the reputation, and the glory of the Almighty to be for a memorial. Lot was with Abram, and he had flocks, herds, and tents. Because their substance was great, the land was not able to support them so they could establish themselves and dwell together. Also, concerning law and order, there was a multitude of controversy, quarrels, and contentions between the herdsmen of Abram's cattle and the herdsmen of Lot's cattle. Abram spoke onto Lot saying, I pray that you let there be no controversy, disputing, or contentions between me and you nor between my herdsmen and your herdsmen because we are brethren. Is not the whole land before you? I hope you will separate yourself from me. If you will take the northside, then I will go to the southside. If you depart to the right side, then I will go to the left side. Lot lifted up his eyes, and saw all the plain of Jordan (**Yair-dain**) well-watered everywhere, like the holy land of the Almighty. All the plain of Jordan (**Yair-dain**) was well watered like the fields and wilderness of Egypt as you come onto Zoar (**Zo-air or So-air**). Then Lot chose all the plain of Jordan (**Yair-dain**) for himself. Abram and Lot separated themselves from one another and Lot journeyed east. Abram dwelled in the land of Canaan, and Lot dwelled in the cities of the plain of Jordan (**Yair-dain**). Lot pitched his tent toward the city of Sodom (**Seh-dome**). The men of Sodom were men of mankind. They were blood-thirsty men. They were evil and vicious. Their thoughts were wrong about the Almighty and they thought evil against Him. Their actions caused great amounts of adversity, misery, calamity, trouble, distress, injury, and unhappiness. These men were criminals in the sight of the Almighty because they had sinned to a great degree. The Almighty accounted them as sinful and now they were carrying the blame and condemnation for great offending the Almighty. After Lot separated from Abram, the Almighty spoke onto Abram saying, now, lift up your eyes and look from the place where you are. Look northward, southward, eastward, and westward. All the fields and wilderness and open land you are gazing upon, you have foreseen by vision. You have My command upon you and I have given this land to you to occupy. I have observed and considered the children of your semen, the descendants of your offspring onto the end of your posterity, and I will extend MY compassion. The Almighty continued speaking and promised Abram saying, I have appointed this land to children of your semen, to descendants of your offspring and to the last of your posterity onto certain descendants of moral quality. Of your posterity, I have appointed this land to a practitioner of MY righteousness forever. To be for a sign, I have ordained and appointed a set of descendants from your offspring to become a nation. They will commit to care for and rehearse My command and My Covenant in the land. I will put My charge upon them to constitute. To be for a sign, at the end of your posterity, I have ordained descendants from your posterity to become a nation of returning exiles. I will preserve them and I will transform them who are of moral quality. I will fix them for My purpose. They will commit to honoring and executing My charge. They will rehearse and care for My charge. They will constitute My charge. I will establish My commandments with them, then I will cause these descendants of your posterity to become like the dust of the Earth, so if a man could number the dust of the Earth, this is how you will number your descendants.

ow arise and walk through the land in the length of it, and in the width of it because I have l given it to you. Then Abram removed his tent from that place and departed. He came into Hebron (**Hev-rone**) and dwelt in the plain of Mamre (**Mam-ray**). He set up and built an altar there to honor the Almighty. Now, Amraphel (**am-rah-phel**) was the king of Shinar in Babylonia. Arioch (**air-re-oak**) was the king of Ellasar (**El-lah-sar**) in Babylonia. Chedorlaomer (**Ked-door-lah-o-mare**) was the king of Elam (**Ay-lam**). He was in a place east of Babylon. Tidal (**Tid-al**) was a Canaanite king of different gentile nations. In the days of their living, it came to pass. These kings dress themselves for engaging in warfare. They prepared their warriors for fighting a battle and they made wars. They made war against Bera (**Beh-rhakh**). Bera is the king of Sodom (**Seh-dome**). Bera was a son of evil. They made war against Birsha (**Beer-shakh**). Birsha is the king of Gomorrah (**Am-mo-rah**). He satisfied himself by wickedness. They made war against Shinab (**Shin-av**). Shinab was the Canaanite king of Admah (**Ad-mah**). They made war against Shemeber (**Shem-ay-vair**). Shemeber was the king of Zeboim (**sev-vah-eem**). They made war against Bela (**Bel-lakh**). Bela was king of Zoar (**Tso-air**). So, Amraphel, Arioch, Chedorlaomer, and Tidal were all kings joined together as allies. These kings made war against Bera, Birsha, Shinab, Shemeber, and Bela who also were all kings joined together as allies. They were all tied to the charms of magic. These two alliances of kings came to battle each other in the lowland of the open country wherein are the salt pits of the sea. Bera, Birsha, Shinab, Shemeber, and Bela served Chedorlaomer (**Ked-door-lah-o-mare**) for twelve years, and they rebelled in the thirteenth year. In the fourteenth year, Chedorlaomer (**Ked-door-lah-o-mare**) and the kings that were with him came, and attacked the Rephaims (**Raph-pha-ee**). The Rephaims (**Raph-pha-ee**), were an old tribe of giants. They were killed in Ashteroth (**Ash-ter-roath**) Karnaim (**care-nigh-im**). Chedorlaomer (**Ked-door-lah-o-mare**) and the kings that were with him came, and attacked the Zuzims (**Zu-zeem**). The Zuzims were in the country of Ham (Kham), and they were slaughtered. Chedorlaomer (**Ked-door-lah-o-mare**) and the kings that were with him came, and attacked the Emims (**Ay-meem**). The Emims (**Ay-meem**) were in Shaveh (**Shah-veh**) Kiriathaim (**Keer-ee-ath-ah-eem**), and they were slaughtered. Chedorlaomer (**Ked-door-lah-o-mare**) and the kings that were with him came and attacked the Horites (**Khore-ee**). The Horites were slaughtered in the mountains and hills of Seir (**Say-eer**). They continued their attack on the Horites and slaughtered their mighty ones, their leaders, and nobles who were in the city state of Elparan (**ale-pah-ron**). Based on their relationship to the people, based on their spirituality, Chedorlaomer and the kings that were with him turned back and came to Eyn (**ak-en**). Eyn is of Kadesh. Chedorlaomer (**Ked-door-lah-o-mare**) and the kings that were with him attacked all the land of Amalekite (**am-mah-lay-kee**). The Amalekite were slaughtered. Chedorlaomer (**Ked-door-lah-o-mare**) and the kings that were with him attacked the Amorites (**Em-mor-ee**). The Amorites were a Canaanite people who lived in Hazezontamar (**Hatz-on-tah-mar**). The Amorites were slaughtered.

In the valley of Siddim (**Sah-deem**), in the lowland of the open country wherein are the salt pits of the sea, Bera, king of Sodom, Birsha, king of Gommorah, Shinab, king of Admah, Shemeber, king of Zeboim and, king Bela of Zoar engage in war against Chedorlaomer, (**Ked-door-lah-o-mare**), the king of Elam, Tidal, (**Tid-al**), a Canaanite (**Ken-an-ah-nee**) king of different gentile nations, Amraphel, (**am-rah-phel**), king of Shinar, and against Arioch (**air-re-oak**), king of Ellasar (**El-lah-sar**). Chedorlaomer, Tidal, Amraphel, and Arioch against Bera, Birsha, Shinab, Shemeber, and Bela. It was four kings against five, and the valley of Siddim was full of slime pits. The king of Sodom and the king of Gomorrah tried to flee and escape, but they were attacked and died violent deaths. They were inferior, therefore, they were overthrown and cast down. Those of them that remained fled on horseback to the mountains and they escaped. Chedorlaomer and the kings that were with him took possession of all the riches, all the food supplies, and all the goods in Sodom (**Seh-dome**) and Gomorrah (**Am-mo-rah**), then they went their way. They took possession of Lot, Abram's brother's son who lived in Sodom. They took possession of Lot's goods, his food, and riches, then they departed away. There came one of those who fled and escaped. He came onto Abram. Abram was a Hebrew (**Ev-ree**) man. He was a descendant of Eber (**Ay-vair**). Abram lived in the plain of Mamre (**Mam-ray**), the Amorite (**Em-mor-ee**). Mamray was brother of Eschol (**Ash-coal**), an Amorite dwelling in the valley of Eschol (**Ash-coal**). Eschol was the brother of Aner (**i-nair**). Aner was the leader of the Amorite. These rulers and lords were sworn to foreign gods but they all pledged their friendship and made an alliance with Abram. They pledged friendship with the Almighty. They made an agreement to keep the Covenant of the Almighty from being violated. Now, one of the persons who escaped spoke to Abram. Abram listened and understood what was declared onto him, that his brother's son Lot was captured and carried away. Abram armed his trained servants. Altogether, they were a total of three hundred eighteen. Abram and his servants pursued after Lot onto the northern city of Dan (**Dawn**). By night, Abram assigned divisions among himself. Then, he and his servants attacked the enemy and killed them. Abram pursued them onto Hobah (**Ho-vah**). Hobah is a city north of Damascus (**Dam-mah-sek**). Abram brought back all the goods and riches. Abram brought his brother's son Lot back along with Lot's goods and riches. Abram brought back the women and people who were captured and carried away. After Abram returned from the slaughter of Chedorlaomer (**Ked-door-lah-o-mare**), and from the slaughter of the kings that were with him, the new king of Sodom went out to meet him in the valley of Shaveh (**Shah-vay**). Melchizedek (**Mal-kee-zed-ik**), a priest-king of Salem (**Shah-lame**) brought Abram bread and wine. Melchizedek was the priest-king of the most high god of the Eloheem. Melchizedek praised and adored Abram. Melchizedek declared saying, praise and adoration be to Abram from the most high god of the Eloheem who is possessor of heaven and earth. Praise and adoration be to the most high god of the Eloheem, who has delivered your enemies into your hand. Then, Melchizedek (**Mal-kee-zed-ik**) gave Abram tithes of all he had. The king of Sodom spoke onto Abram saying, give me the people. Take the goods and riches for yourself. Abram answered, saying, I have offered my strength, my power, and my fellowship. I have contributed my hands to the service of the Almighty. The Almighty is higher above angel-princes. The Almighty is higher than the most high god of the Eloheem. I serve the Almighty.

The Almighty is the All Supreme Being. The Almighty is the All Supreme Ruler. The Almighty is the Creator of all things. The Almighty is the first Possessor and Originator of the Earth, its Heavens, and all its inhabitants. Therefore, I will not take a thread from Melchizedek (**Mal-kee-zed-ik**), and I will not take a thread from a shoe-latchet from you. I will not take any thing that is yours because you might say, I have made Abram rich. Apart from what the young men have eaten, give a portion to the men that went with me including Aner (**i-nair**), Eshcol (**Ash-coal**), and Mamre (**Mam-ray**). Let them take possession of their portion. After these things, the Almighty communicated with Abram. The Almighty visited Abram, and talked to him in a vision saying, do not be inspired nor put in fear by morals of the godly. Do not be inspired nor made afraid by the honor and respect persons give to those of godly morals. Abram, do not fear their terrible acts. I, the Almighty, the All Supreme Being, the All Supreme Ruler, am your ruler and protector. I am your weapon and shield of defense. I am the greatest worth. I am the greatest degree of greatness. I pay the highest price for hire. I pay the greatest wages for service. I give the greatest benefits and rewards. Abram responded to the Almighty asking, what will You give me seeing that I live according to Your manners, seeing I travel abroad to and from places speaking of Your customs? What will you give me knowing I am destitute of children? I am childless and the heir of my house, this Eliezer (**ale-ee-aye-zair**) of Damascus (**Dam-mah-sek**) is a servant-steward, a son by possession. In the vision, Abram continued speaking to the Almighty saying, look and see, physically you have granted me no children for descendants. Physically, you have not given me a child of my semen, yet look and see, a certain servant born in my house is my heir. He is my son by possession. Then, the Almighty responded to him saying, your servant will disinherit. He will be brought to ruin. He will take possession of poverty and be impoverished. He will not be your heir, but he that will come forth from your own semen will inherit your possessions. He that will come forth from your own semen will be your heir. In the vision, the Almighty took Abram outdoors, out of the streets, out of the fields, outward, and abroad, then spoke to him saying, now look toward the heaven and consider. As a learned man, as a learned scribe, take account of the shining stars that rule over the stargazers. As a learned scribe, record the number of shining stars. Count the stars that are personified by the Eloheem to be an all knowing god-king, his family, and his progeny. As a learned scribe, count their number in totality, and declare them accurately. If you can number them, the Almighty told Abram, this is what the number of descendants from your posterity will be. Abram considered that the Almighty nourished him. The Almighty cared for him. The Almighty had established him. The words that came from the Almighty assured him. Abram trusted in the Almighty and remained faithful without fail. He believed in the Almighty. Abram believed the Almighty is the All Supreme Being. Abram believed the Almighty is the All Supreme Ruler. Abram believed the Almighty is the Creator of all things. As the Almighty had imagined and devised, as the Almighty predicted, the Almighty counted Abram's belief as righteous. The Almighty counted Abram as a righteous king of righteous judgment who will perform justice that is righteous. The Almighty counted Abram being righteous according to His law and truth, therefore, the Almighty justified Abram. The Almighty continued speaking to Abram saying, I am the Almighty the All Supreme Being, the All Supreme Ruler, the Creator of all things.

brought you out of southern Babylonia, out of the city-state of Ur (**oo-ore**). Ur is a city of moon worship in Chaldee (**Cas-dee**) of the Chaldeans. I brought you away from that land of your kindred to give you this land to inherit. Abram asked the Almighty, how long, and how will I know when I can confess that I have taken possession of the land as an inheritance? Then, Almighty answered Abram and spoke onto him saying, to your altar, bring ME one heifer of three years old, one she goat of three years old, one ram of three years old, one turtledove, and one nestling bird with no feathers. Abram got these animals for the Almighty, then he cut them in the middle, and laid each piece one against another on the altar, but Abram did not cut the birds. When the vultures came down upon the dead bodies of animals, Abram drove them away. When the sun was going down, a deep sleep fell upon Abram. As Abram slept, a great darkness and misery fell upon him. Abram saw fear, terror, fright, dread, and the horror of terrible idols. After the sun went down and it was dark, Abram awoke. When Abram lifted his eyes, he saw the Almighty passing between those pieces of animal flesh he had cut up and offered on the altar. Passing between those pieces of animal flesh, the Almighty was like a torch of burning flames and smoke. Passing between those pieces of animal flesh, the Almighty was like an oven of smoke and fiery hot flames. Then the Almighty spoke onto Abram, saying, consider what has been revealed to you. Instruct others on these things and make these things known. Of surety, of this age, you have seen your descendants to the end of their generations. You know that the descendants of your posterity will serve a stranger in a land that is not theirs. These strangers will oppress them, humiliate them, ravish them, defile them, afflict them, and deal cruelly with them for four hundred years. At the end of that time, that nation, whom they will serve, I will judge and execute judgment upon. Afterward, your descendants will come out with great amounts of goods, riches, and possessions. Abram, you will be counted with the respect and honor of your forefathers who had the peace and friendship of My Covenant. You will be counted with the respect and honor of your forefathers who had peace from war, who had peace in their relationships, who had health, who had prosperity, and who were completely safe. You will be buried in a good old age. But in the fourth generation your descendants will come here again because the iniquity of the Amorites is not yet full. The Almighty continued speaking then made a Covenant of peace and friendship with Abram. The Almighty spoke to him saying, I have given this land onto your children, onto their descendants, onto their descendants, and onto the descendants of your posterity. From the river of Egypt onto the great river of Euphrates including the Kenites (**Kay-nee**). They are a Canaanite people. The Kenizzites (**Kay-nee-zee**), they are descendants of Kenaz. The Kadmonites (**Kad-mo-nee**). The Hittites (**Hayth**). They are descendants of Heth (**Hayth**). Heth is the second son of Canaan. The Perizzites (**Pear-rah-zee**). They are Canaanites of the open country. The Rephaims (**Ref-pha-ee**). They are an old tribe of giants. The Amorites (**Em-mor-ee**). All the Canaanites (**Ken-nah, a-nee**). The Girgashites (**Gear-gah-she**). The Jebusites (**Yev-vu-see**). Now Sarai (**Sar-rye**), Abram's wife had no children. She had a handmaid, an Egyptian (**Mitz-rye-em**), whose name was Hagar (**Hah-gar**). Hagar had the reputation, the honor, the authority, and the glory of a slave girl. Sarai spoke to Abram saying, now, look, the Almighty has stopped me from given birth to a child. I am under HIS restraint. I pray that you go in onto my maid with sexual affections.

It could be that I can have children by her. I could be a mother by possession. Abram listened and understood. He agreed and obeyed the voice of his wife Sarai. After Abram had been living ten years in the land of Canaan, Sarai, Abram's wife took her handmaid Hagar (**Hah-gar**), the Egyptian (**Mitz-rye-em**), and gave her to her husband Abram to have a child. Abram did son, and, Hagar became his second wife. Abram went in onto Hagar with sexual affections. He presented himself to her and she conceived. When Hagar saw that she had conceived, she began to despise her mistress Sarai, and Sarai, Hagar's mistress, despised Hagar because she became pregnant with Abram's child. Sarai spoke to Abram saying, the wrong of my false dealing is upon you. I have put my handmaid in your lap to embrace your bosom. When Hagar saw that she had conceived, then I became despised in her eyes. Let the Almighty execute HIS judgment between me and her. Abram spoke to Sarai saying, look and see, she is your handmaid. She is under your strength and power. She is in your hand. Do to her as it pleases you. Then, Sarai afflicted and troubled Hagar. Sarai humiliated Hagar and dealt hardly with her. Because of Sarai's oppression, Hagar ran away speedily. Then, by a well of water on the path to Shur (**Shu-er**), a messenger of the Almighty's prophecy found her in the wilderness. He asked Hagar, what brought you here? Where are you going? Hagar answered saying, I am running away from the face of my mistress. The messenger of the Almighty's prophecy responded saying, return to your mistress. Submit yourself under her strength and power. The messenger of the Almighty's prophecy continued speaking onto her saying, the Almighty will greatly multiply the descendants of your child. They will not be counted accurately because it will be a great multitude. The messenger of the Almighty's prophecy said onto her, look, you are with child. You will give birth to a son. You will call his name Ishmael (**Yish-mah-ale**) because the Almighty listens and understands your depression, your misery, your trouble, and your poverty. The child will become a wild man and his power and strength will be against every man. Every man's power and strength will be against him. He will live in the presence of all his brethren. Afterwards, Hagar gave her attention to discern and distinguish what the messenger of the Almighty spoke onto her. After that time, she invited guests then proclaimed and preached the honor, the reputation, the glory, and the authority of the Almighty. Hagar spoke aloud saying, You, Almighty, All Supreme Being, Creator of all things, You considered me, You have watched and observed me to find out if You could respect me. You see my appearance. You see my spectacle and You look at my performance. Here, I have had an experience with You and afterwards I considered Your honor, Your reputation, Your authority, Your glory, and Your character. I have approved of You and I respect You in the sight of others. I have designated this to be an individual memorial to honor You. Therefore, the well was called Beerlahairoi (**Be-air-lah-hi- ro -ee**), the well of the One Living True Supreme Being. The well is west of Kadesh (**Kah-daysh**) between Kadesh and Bered (**Beh-red**). Hagar gave birth to a son for Abram. Abram called his son's name Ishmael. Abram was eighty-six years old when Hagar gave birth to Ishmael. When Abram was ninety-nine years old, the Almighty observed, considered and respected Abram. In a vision, the Almighty appeared visible and presented Himself face to face with Abram. The Almighty spoke to Abram saying, I am the Almighty, the most powerful being, the All Supreme Ruler.

Walk away from gods, godlike ones, and mighty ones because they are false. Do not live in their manner nor lead another to live in their manner of life. Do not walk abroad spreading their manner of life to make it grow greater. Walk away from angels and demons, they are men of rank, mighty heroes, and imaginations. They are purposed to die prematurely. Live according to My command and declare My promise. In My sight, you will be innocent. You will have healthy morals. You will have integrity and truth that is undefiled. You will be perfect without blemish. I have made My Covenant with you. With you, I have made My alliance between mankind and their Maker. I have entrusted you with My friendship. I have appointed you to direct, deliver, and constitute My Law. I have appointed you to keep and perform My Covenant. Abram fell onto his face, then the Almighty promised Abram and spoke to Abram saying, behold, My Covenant is with you and you will be an ancestor of many nations. I am going to make you very powerful. Your honor, your reputation, your glory is chosen no more to be called Abram (**Av-rum**), the exalted king, but for your honor, your reputation, and glory, you are chosen to be called Abraham (**Av-rah-hum**), the ancestral father of multitude because I, the Almighty, have made you an exalted ancestor, an originator of many different nations of people. Between Me and you, I have established My Covenant and My friendship. Between Me and your children, between Me and their descendants, between Me and their posterity, in all their generations I have established My Covenant with them. My Covenant is an everlasting treaty of peace. It is an everlasting alliance. It is an everlasting friendship. It is an everlasting agreement to be your one and only, All Supreme Ruler, and I will be the same All Supreme Ruler onto you, and to your children, onto your children's offspring, onto your children's offspring's' descendants, onto their descendants, onto their descendants posterity, in all their generations forever. The land wherein you are a stranger, I give and entrust to you, and to your children, to your children's offspring, to your children's offsprings' descendants, to their descendants, to their descendants' posterity, in all their generations forever, even all the land of Canaan, for an everlasting inheritance, for an everlasting possession, and, I, the Almighty, the All Supreme Being, the Creator of all things will be their one and only. I will be their All Supreme Ruler. The Almighty continued speaking to Abraham saying, beware, you are My watchman, you will have charge of keeping My Covenant. You, yourself, will watch over and protect My Covenant. You will observe, celebrate, and perform the commands of My Covenant. Your children, your children's offspring, your children's offsprings' descendants, their descendants, onto their descendants' posterity will have charge of keeping My Covenant forever. They, themselves, will watch over and protect My Covenant. They will observe, celebrate, and perform the commands of My Covenant, in their generations forever. This is My Covenant that you will perform, watch over, preserve, and protect. This is My Covenant that your children, your children's offspring, your children's offsprings' descendants, their descendants, onto their descendants' posterity will perform, watch over, preserve, and protect. You, every man, and every man child among you will circumcise their flesh by cutting their foreskin off. This will be a signal and a sign of the Covenant between Me and you. Between Me and them. He among you that is eight days old or older will be circumcised.

Every man, every male among the men, and every man child in your house throughout their generations. You will circumcise him that is born in your house. You will circumcise him that is bought with your money. You will circumcise any stranger joined to your house that is not of your semen. He that is born in your house, and him that is bought with your money must be circumcised in the flesh by cutting their foreskin off because My Covenant will be in your flesh and their flesh for an everlasting Covenant. The man, the human male, and the man child joined to your house who is not circumcised in the flesh, whose foreskin is not cut off, that soul will be cut off from his people because HE has violated and broken My Covenant. The Almighty continued speaking to Abraham saying, as for your wife Sarai, you will no longer call your wife Sarai (**Sar-rhy**). You will no longer call her by the reputation, the honor, the glory, and the authority of a noble princess, but you will call her Sarah (**Sar-rah**). You will call her by the reputation, the honor, the glory, and the authority of a noble queen. I will bless her to be praised and adored. I will give you a son from her. She will be mother of a multitude of people and kings of people will be of her blood. Abraham laughed, then fell upon his face, and considered. In his heart, he asked himself, will a child be born onto him that is one hundred years old? Will Sarah, who is ninety years old, give birth to a child? Abraham spoke to the Almighty, saying, if only Ishmael might live and be preserved in Your sight. The Almighty spoke to Abraham, saying, your wife Sarah will give birth to a son for you. You will call his name Isaac (**Yitz-ac**). I will establish My Covenant with him and it will be an everlasting covenant. I will establish

My Covenant with his children, with his children's offspring, with his children's offspring's' descendants, with their descendants, onto their descendants posterity. As for Ishmael (**Yish-mah-ale**), I have listened with interest and I understand you. Behold, I have blessed him to praised and adored. I will make him fruitful and I will make him become numerous in number. He will father twelve leaders, and I will make him a great nation. But I will establish My Covenant with your son Isaac. Sarah (**Sar-rah**) will give birth to him at this same time next year. Then, the Almighty stopped talking with him. The Almighty ascended up and away from Abraham (**Av-rah-hum**). Abraham and his son Ishmael were circumcised on the same day. Abraham was ninety-nine years old when he was circumcised in the flesh by cutting his foreskin off. Ishmael his son was thirteen years old, when he was circumcised in the flesh by cutting his foreskin off. Every man and every man child born in Abraham's house, all the strangers joined to Abraham's house, and all those who were bought with his money, all the men of Abraham's house were circumcised in the flesh with him by cutting their foreskins off. In the plains of Mamre (**Mam-ray**), in the heat of the day, Abraham sat in his tent's door, in a vision, the Almighty had appeared and was visible before the face of Abraham. Abraham considered that vision of the Almighty appearing visibly before his face. He gave his attention to discern and understand it. Then the Abraham lifted his eyes and beheld three men standing by him. When he saw them, he observed and considered. As they were looking at each other's face, Abraham discerned, he had foresaw one of them in a vision, then he moved quickly from the tent's door and rushed to meet them and help them. Abraham bowed himself humbly with his face toward the ground. Then he spoke saying, now, if I have found favor in your sight, I pray you do not pass by this servant of the Almighty and leave away from out of this land.

Abraham continued speaking saying, I hope you will let me get you all a little water to wash your feet that you journey on. If you trust in the Almighty, you can stay. Now, go rest yourselves under the tree. I will get you all some food and bread. Rest and strengthen your hearts. Rest and comfort your hearts, after that, you can pass on by me to leave out of this land. So tell me, are you passing by this servant of the Almighty and leaving away from out of my land? They answered saying, so do, as you have said. Abraham rushed into the tent to Sarah, and told her to quickly make three measures of fine meal. Knead it into dough, and make cakes of bread upon the fire pot. Abraham moved quickly onto the herd, and got a good tender calf, then gave it to his servant. The young man rushed to prepare it. He took bread, butter, milk, and the calf that he had prepared and set it before them. As the young man stood by them under the tree, they did eat. ONE of them asked Abraham, where is your wife Sarah? Abraham answered saying, in the tent, look and see. That same ONE of them said, your wife Sarah will have a son. According to that child's time of life, I will certainly return to you. Sarah heard their voices. She listened with interest behind them in the tent's door. Now Abraham and Sarah were old in age and well stricken. This ceased to be with Sarah, her giving birth in the custom of women. Therefore, Sarah laughed within herself asking, will I have this delight, after I have grown to be old, my husband being old also? The Almighty, who is the ONE of those men, asked Abraham, why did Sarah laugh, saying, will I of certainty give birth to a child now that I am old? Is anything too hard for the Almighty, the All Supreme Being, the Creator of all things? Sarah will give birth to a son. I will return to you, at the appointed time, according to that child's time of life. Because she had respect and honor for the Almighty, Sarah was astonished, and afraid. Sarah denied laughing by saying, I did not laugh. The Almighty spoke to her saying, no, but you did laugh. The men rose up from there and looked toward Sodom with interest. Abraham went with them to bring them on the way. And the Almighty spoke to Himself saying, will I keep the thing I am doing a secret from Abraham? Seeing that Abraham is a chief ancestor of them that will surely become a great and mighty nation of people. I have made all the nations of the earth be blessed through him and I will make all nations of the earth be blessed through his posterity? As I foresaw, as I learned to know him, it was revealed to Me. I know he will command his children and his household after him. They will watch over and protect the way of the Almighty. They will preserve, observe, and perform the way of the Almighty. They will perform My Law righteously. They will execute justice and execute judgment righteously so I, the Almighty, will bring upon Abraham that which has been promised to him. Then, the Almighty spoke to Abraham, saying, the sin and the guiltiness of Sodom and Gomorrah is being glorified and promoted in honor. The sin of Sodom and Gomorrah is very grievous and their outcry is very great. They are enjoying their sin. They are enjoying honor from being guilty, and that honor is gaining great glory. Therefore, I declared, saying now, I will go down to see them altogether whether they have done according to their outcry that is come onto ME, and if not, I will know. From there, the men turned their faces away from Abraham and went toward Sodom, yet Abraham continued to stand before the ONE of them who was Almighty. Abraham drew near and asked, will You destroy the wicked along with the righteous, who are lawful in character?

Will You destroy those with good morals along with those who are morally wrong and hostile against You? If there be fifty righteous within the city, will You not spare the place for the sake of the fifty righteous that are there in it? To kill the righteous along with the wicked, this is a thing very far away from You to do. Treating the righteous the same as the wicked is also a thing very far away from You to do. Will not the Judge of all the earth do what is right? The Almighty answered Abraham saying, if I find fifty righteous within the city of Sodom, then I will spare all their places for their sakes. Abraham responded saying, now, I am only dust and ashes, but I have taken it upon myself to speak to the Almighty, the All Supreme Ruler, the Creator of all things. If there be forty-five righteous in the city will You destroy all the city for lack of five righteous persons? The Almighty answered, if I find forty-five righteous persons there, then I will not destroy all of it. Abraham spoke to the Almighty again saying, what if there will be forty righteous persons found there. The Almighty responded, I will not destroy it all for the forty's sake. Abraham spoke to the Almighty saying, I will speak, oh let not the All Supreme Ruler be angry. If thirty righteous persons be found there. The Almighty answered saying, if I find thirty righteous persons there, I will not destroy it all. Abraham spoke to the Almighty saying, now, I have taken it upon myself to speak to the Almighty. If twenty righteous persons be found there. The Almighty answered saying, I will not destroy it all for the sake of twenty righteous persons. Abraham spoke to the Almighty saying, I will speak one more time, oh let not the Almighty be angry. If ten righteous persons be found there, and the Almighty answered saying, I will not destroy it all for the sake of ten righteous persons. As soon as the Almighty stopped communing with Abraham, the Almighty went HIS own way, and Abraham returned to his own place. At the evening, two messengers of the Almighty came into Sodom. Abraham's nephew Lot sat in the entrance gate of Sodom. When the messengers appeared visible. Lot considered and looked at them to distinguish them. He observed them. As they looked at one another, foreseeing an experience with them, Lot rose up to meet them and help them. Lot humbly bowed himself with his face toward the ground. Lot spoke to them saying, as servants of the Almighty, the All Supreme Ruler, remove yourselves from rebellion. As worshippers of the Almighty, turn away from wickedness. Now, I pray that you turn in and come to my house where you will stay. You can wash your feet and rest all night. You will rise up early and go your way. They answered Lot saying, we will stay in the streets all night long. Lot urged them greatly not to stay in the streets of the city and they hearkened. They turned in to him. They entered into Lot's house. Lot prepared them a feast and baked unleavened bread. They did eat. Before they lay down to sleep, the men of Sodom surrounded the house all around. Both young and old, they were all men of mankind. All the men from every quarter of the city. They called on the reputation and honor of Lot. They spoke to him asking, where are the men that came in to your house this night? Bring them out to us, so we can become acquainted with them, so we can make ourselves known to them. Bring them out to us, so we can physically know them and they can physically know us. Lot went out the door to them and shut the door behind himself. Lot spoke to them saying, my brethren, I pray you do not be evil and act so wickedly. Now, I have two daughters that have not known a man.

I hope you will let me bring them out onto you, and you can do whatever you think is good to them. You can do to them whatever your soul tells you is good, only do nothing to these men because they are under the protection of my roof. They answered Lot saying, you stand back. At least one of those fellows that came here to sojourn needs to be a judged now or we will deal worse with you than with them. They pressed sore upon the man even upon Lot, and they came near to break down the door. But the two messengers of the Almighty in Lot's home used the strength and power of their hands to pull Lot into the house to them, and, they shut the door behind him. Then, the Sodomites at the door of the house were struck with blindness so that they were grieved. They exhausted themselves trying to find the door. The messengers of the Almighty spoke to Lot asking, have you any other family here? If you have a son in law, sons, daughters, or whatever you have in the city, bring them out of this place because the Almighty is going to destroy this place. The outcry of them in this city has grown to be great against the Almighty. The honor given to their outcry against the Almighty has grown to be great. Therefore, the Almighty, the All Supreme Ruler is going to destroy this city of excitement, terror, and anguish. When the morning arose, the messengers of the Almighty were rushing Lot and spoke to him saying, take your wife, and your two daughters that are here out of this city otherwise you'll be consumed along with the sin of this city. Lot went out and spoke to his sons-in-law saying, you get up and you get out of this city because the Almighty is going to destroy it. But to them, Lot seemed like one that mocked. Now, Lot began lingering and delaying himself. Because the Almighty was merciful to Lot, the messengers of the Almighty laid hold onto his hand, and onto the hand of his wife, and onto the hand of his two daughters, and they brought them forth, and set them outside the city. It came to pass, when the messengers of the Almighty had brought them forth and set them abroad, they spoke to Lot saying, run for your life. Do not look behind yourselves and do not stay in all this plain. Escape to the mountain, otherwise you'll be killed. Lot responded saying, oh, not so, my fellow servant of the Almighty. Now, I have found grace in your sight, and you have magnified your mercy that you have showed onto me by saving my life, but I cannot escape to the mountain unless some evil take me and I die prematurely. I cannot escape to the mountain unless some evil take me and I am put to death by a magician of necromancy. I cannot escape to the mountain unless some evil take me and I am executed by a warlock of necromancy. Look and see. There is a city near to me where I can escape to, and it is a little one. Is it not a little one? Oh let me escape there, and I will live my life. One of the two messengers spoke to Lot saying, the Almighty has accepted you concerning your request, so He will not overthrow that city you have spoken of. Now, run away to escape there because nothing will be done until you make it there. The name of the city was called Zoar (**Tso-air**). The sun had risen upon the earth when Lot entered into Zoar. Then, from out of heaven, the Almighty rained brimstone and fire upon Sodom and upon Gomorrah. The Almighty overthrew those cities of the plain, and, all the inhabitants of the cities. Lot's wife looked back behind herself, and she became a statue of salt. Abraham had gotten up early in that morning and went back to the place where he stood before the Almighty. Abraham looked toward Sodom, Gomorrah, and toward all the land of the plain. Like smoke coming out of a furnace, Abraham saw smoke going up from the land.

It came to pass, when the Almighty destroyed the cities of the plain, He remembered Abraham, and when He overthrew the cities where Lot dwelt, the Almighty sent Lot out of the midst of the overthrow. Lot went up out of Zoar and lived in the mountain. His two daughters were with him. Lot was scared to live in Zoar. Because of his fear, he lived in a cavern in the mountains, he and his two daughters. Lot's firstborn daughter spoke to the younger saying, our father is old and in all the Earth, there is not a man to come in onto us that will follow after our moral character. In all the Earth, there is not a man to come in onto us that will follow after our habits and way of living. Come, let us make our father drink wine, then we will lie with him so we can preserve the seed of our father. That night, they made their father drink wine and the firstborn went in and laid with her father in sexual relations. Lot was not aware and did not consider. He did not know when she laid down with him in sexual relations nor was he aware when she arose. And it came to pass, on the next day, the firstborn spoke to the younger saying, look, you saw last night. I laid with my father in sexual relations. This night, let us make him drink wine also, then you go in and lie with him in sexual relations so we can preserve the seed of our father. That night, they made their father drink wine also, then his younger daughter arose and lay with him in sexual relations. Lot was not aware and did not consider. He did not know when she laid down with him in sexual relations nor was he aware when she arose. Thus, both daughters of Lot were with child by their father. The firstborn gave birth to a son and called his name Moab. The same is the ancestral father of the Moabites onto this day. The younger daughter, she also gave birth to a son. She called his name Benammi (**Ben-am-mee**). The same is the ancestral father of the children of Ammon (Am-moan) onto this day. From there, Abraham journeyed toward the south country and dwelled between Kadesh (**Kah-daysh**) and Shur (**Shu-ore**), then he sojourned in Gerar (**Geh-rar**), a Philistine town south of Gaza (**Azz-sah**). Abraham spoke of his wife Sarah saying, she is my sister. Abimelech (**Ave-vee-mel-lakh**), king of Gerar sent for Sarah and took possession of Sarah. By night, in an ordinary dream, the Almighty came to Abimelech and spoke to him, warning him saying, look and see, you are but a dead man because the woman that you have carried off and taken possession of is another man's wife. Now, Abimelech (**Ave-vee-mel-lakh**) had not come near to Sarah sexually and he answered saying, my master, will You kill a righteous nation? Did not Abraham tell me, she is my sister? She, even she herself spoke and declared, saying, he is my brother. I have done this of my heart with perfect integrity. My hands are innocent. In this dream, the Almighty continued speaking to him saying, yes, I know that you did this of your heart with perfect integrity because I withheld you from sinning against Me. I, the Almighty did not put it upon you to touch her. Now, bring Abraham's wife back to him because he is MY prophet. He speaks and declares My prophecies and he will judge you. If he prays for you, then you will live. If you do not bring his wife back to him, then you know, as a penalty of neglecting wise conduct and good morals, you and all that is yours will die prematurely. Suddenly, you all will be put to death. You will be killed by a warlock magician of necromancy and your nation will perish. Early in the morning, Abimelech arose and called all his servants. He told all those things in their ears and the men were terrified and very afraid of seeing those terrible things. Abimelech (**Ave-vee-mel-lakh**) called for Abraham and spoke to him asking, what have you done to us?

How and when have I offended you? What did I do to make you bring a great sin onto me and onto my kingdom? Your actions and the things you have done toward me should not be done. Abimelech spoke to Abraham asking, what have you observed, what have you seen that made you do this thing? Abraham answered because I thought for certainty, the fear of the Almighty, the fear of His terror, and the respect of His morals is not in this place, therefore, you will kill me to take my wife for yourself. Yet, indeed, she is a sister of my nation of people and she is my adopted sister. She is not the daughter of my mother. She is the adopted daughter of my father and she became my wife. It came to pass, when the Almighty caused me to journey away from my father's house, that I spoke to her and commanded, saying, this is your kindness that you will show onto me at every place we will come to, you speak of me, saying, he is my brother. Abimelech took sheep, oxen, menservants, and women servants, then he gave them to Abraham, and restored his wife Sarah back onto him. Abimelech (**Ave-vee-mel-lec**) spoke, saying, look and see, my land is in front of you, live where it pleases you. Onto Sarah he spoke, saying, look and see, I have given your brother one thousand pieces of silver. Look and see, he is to you a covering of the eyes, onto all that are with you, and with all others, thus, she was corrected. Because of Abraham's wife Sarah, the Almighty had quickly closed up all the wombs of the house of Abimelech. Abraham mediated and prayed onto the Almighty and the Almighty, the All Supreme Being, the Creator of all things healed Abimelech's house, his wife, his maidservants, and they gave birth to children. The Almighty kept Sarah in His remembrance and He cared for her. He paid attention to her and watched over her as the Almighty had appointed as He had spoken. The Almighty did onto Sarah as He had spoken. At the set time that the Almighty had spoken to Abraham, Sarah conceived, then she brought forth a son, who was of Abraham. It came to pass, when this happened, Abraham was in his old age. Abraham chose and invited guests to preach to them. Abraham preached to them about the Almighty. Abraham brought his son before his guests and declared him to be of his own lineage and call his name Isaac (**Yitz-ac**). Sarah spoke to the guests saying, the Almighty has caused me to laugh merrily so that all that hear me will laugh merrily with me. Sarah continued speaking, saying, who would have spoken to Abraham saying, Sarah should have given you a baby. Can Sarah be a nursing mother? Because in his old age and in my own old age, I have conceived by him and I have given birth to a son for him. As the Almighty had commanded, being eight days old, Abraham circumcised the flesh of his son Isaac by cutting the foreskin off his flesh. Abraham was one hundred years old when his son Isaac was born onto him. At that time, it came to pass, that Abimelech (**Ave-vee-mel-lec**) and Phichol (**Pee-kohl**) spoke to Abraham. Phichol is a Phillistine. He is the chief captain of Abimelech's host of soldiers. Abimelech spoke to Abraham saying, the Almighty is with you in everything that you do. Now, here, take an oath with me by the Almighty that you will not deal falsely with me nor with my son, nor with my son's son, but according to the kindness that I have done to you, you will do to me, and you will do onto the land where you have lived in. Abraham responded saying, I will take an oath. Abraham corrected Abimelech because of a well of water that Abimelech's servants had violently taken away. Abimelech spoke to Abraham saying, you did not tell me. I was not the one who has appointed this thing, neither have I heard about it until today.

Abraham took some of his sheep and oxen then gave them to Abimelech, then both of them made a friendship, an alliance, and a covenant between one another. Abraham set seven young lambs of the flock by themselves. Abimelech spoke to Abraham asking, what do the seven young lambs that you have set by themselves mean? Abraham answered saying, for these seven young lambs that I give you out of my hand, they will be a witness to me and you that I have dug this water well. Abraham called that place, Beersheba (**Bay-air-shah-bah**), because there he and Abimelech took an oath. They made a friendship, an alliance, a covenant at Beersheba, then Abimelech and Phichol rose up and returned into the land of the Philistines. Abraham planted a grove of tamarisk trees in Beersheba, then there he chose guests and he invited guests to preach to them the everlasting authority, the reputation, the honor, the glory, and the character of the Almighty. Abraham lived in the Philistines' land many days. Now, Isaac was nourished in body, in mind and he grew to be very strong. He showed he was able to do good and deal rightly on his own. He showed he was able to give out what is good and right on his own. Because of this, Abraham prepared a great feast. At the feast, Sarah saw Ishmael, the son of Hagar the Egyptian, who Hagar gave birth to for Abraham. Sarah observed him and considered. She saw him mocking Isaac and uses him as a toy. She spoke to Abraham saying, throw this maid-servant and her son out. The son of this maid-servant will not be heir with my son Isaac. Sarah's judgment and this matter were very displeasing in the sight of Abraham and it grieved Abraham because of his son. Then the Almighty visited Abraham. He spoke to Abraham saying, do not be displeased because of the boy and his mother. In all that Sarah has spoken to you, listen to her voice and obey what she is saying. I, the Almighty have chosen Isaac. It is Isaac's seed that carries your descendants of moral quality. It is Isaac's seed that carries your descendants who will be summoned to proclaim the important things of the Almighty. From your son Ishmael because he is your child, I, the Almighty, will make a great nation of Gentile people from him. Abraham rose up early in the morning. He took some food, bread, and a bottle of water, then gave it to Hagar. Abraham put the bag on her shoulder along with her child Ishmael, then Abraham sent them away. Hagar departed and wandered in the wilderness of Beersheba (**Bay-air-shah-bah**). Now, the water in her bottle was gone. She placed her child under one of the shrubs. She went and sat down opposite to him a short way off. Hagar spoke to herself saying, let me not see the death of my child. As she sat over opposite to him, Hagar raised her voice and wept. The Almighty heard the voice of the boy and his mother, then like His voice was speaking from the sky He called out to Hagar and spoke to her saying, Hagar do not be troubled. I have considered your voice. I have heard your cry. I have heard the cry of the boy. Do not fear. Arise and lift the boy up. Hold him in your arms because I, the Almighty, will make him become a great nation of Gentile people. Then the Almighty opened her eyes and caused her be observant. Hagar saw a well of water. She went and filled the bottle with water, then gave the boy a drink of water. The Almighty watched over Hagar's boy and the boy grew to become strong. The boy lived in the wilderness. He became an archer and the bow was his strength. He lived in a place of caverns, in the wilderness of Paran (**Pah-run**).

For his possession, his mother got him a wife from out the land of Egypt. Now, Abraham lived in Beersheba. After these things, it came to pass and it was told to Abraham saying, look, Milcah (**Mil-cah**), she has given birth to children for your brother Nahor (**Nah-hore**). His firstborn is Huz (**ootz**), then, Buz (**Booze**), and Kemuel (**Kim-mu-ale**). Kemuel fathered Aram (**Ahr-ram**). Nahor fathered Chesed (**Keh-sed**). Nahor fathered Hazo (**Hahk-zo**). Nahor fathered Pildash (**Pil-dahsh**). Nahor fathered Jidlaph (**Yid-laph**). Nahor fathered Bethuel (**Beth-thu-ale**). Milcah gave birth to these eight for Abraham's brother Nahor. Bethuel fathered Rebekah (**Rev-cah**). Nahor had a concubine who was a Syrian woman, and her name is Reumah (**Reh-oo-mah**). For Nahor, Reumah gave birth to Tebah (**Teh-vakh**), then to Gaham (**Gahk -hem**), then to Thahash (**Takh-hash**), then to Maachah (**Makh-ak-hah**). As a penalty for neglecting wise conduct and good morals, Sarah died prematurely. Suddenly, she was put to death. She was killed in Kirjatharba (**Keer-yath**) (**Air-bah**), in the land of Canaan, after its conquest the same city is called Hebron (**Hev-roan**). Sarah was put to death by a warlock magician of necromancy. Abraham came to mourn for Sarah. He wept for her. Stirred up, Abraham stood up from in front of Sarah's dead body, he stood firm, then, he spoke to the sons of Heth (**Haith**), he spoke to those Hittites saying, I am a stranger and a traveler among you. Give me possession of a burying place among you, so I can bury my dead out of my sight. One of the children of Heth answered Abraham saying, my lord, listen and hear us, you are a mighty king among us. In choosing any of our burial places to bury your dead, none of us will stop you from the burial place you choose. Standing up, Abraham humbly bowed himself to the people of the land and to the sons of Heth. Abraham communed with them saying, if it is set in your mind that I can bury my dead out of my sight, listen and hear me, and be an intercessor for me, between me and the Hittite Ephron (**Eff-roan**), the son of Zohar (**tso-hair**), so he may give me the cave of Machpelah (**Makh-pay-lah**) that he has at the end of his field. He will give it to me for a possession and for a burying place among you, for as much money as it is worth. Ephron lived among the sons of Heth. In an audience of the sons of Heth and of all that went into the gate entrance of his city, Ephron the Hittite (**Haith-ee**) answered Abraham saying, hear me, my lord, I will give you the field, and the cave that is there in it. I give it to you, in the presence of the sons of my people. I give it to you give for a possession and for a burial place to bury your dead. Abraham humbly bowed himself down in front of the people of the land. In the audience of the people of the land, Abraham spoke to Ephron (**Eff-roan**), saying, I pray that you listen to me, if you give it to me, I will give you money for the field. Take the money from me, and I will bury my dead there. Ephron answered Abraham saying, listen to me my lord, the land is worth four hundred shekels of silver. What is that between me and you? With that, you can bury your dead. Abraham listened to Ephron, then Abraham weighed out the amount of silver that Ephron called out in the audience of the sons of Heth. In the current money of the merchant, it was four hundred shekels of silver onto Ephron. The field of Ephron was in Machpelah (**Makh-pay-lah**). Machpelah is before Mamre. The field, all the trees that were in the field, the cave that is there in it and all the borders round-about were guaranteed onto Abraham in the presence of the sons of Heth, and before all that went into the gate entrance of his city.

After this, Abraham buried his wife Sarah in the cave of the field of Machpelah before Mamre (**Mam-ray**) in the land of Canaan (**Ken-ah-an**). Abraham grew older in age, and the Almighty had blessed Abraham in all things and the Almighty blessed Abraham to be greatly loved and greatly praised. Abraham spoke to the eldest servant of his house. This servant ruled over all that he had. Abraham spoke to him saying, put your hand on top of my thigh. I will make you take an oath by the Almighty, the All Supreme Being, the All Supreme Ruler, the Creator of all things that you will not get my son a woman to wife from the daughters of the Canaanites from among where I live. You will go to my relatives in my native land and take a woman to be a wife onto my son Isaac. The servant answered Abraham asking him, what if the woman will not be willing to follow me onto this land? Do I need to bring your son with me to the land from where you come from? Abraham spoke to him saying, beware, that you do not take my son back there. The Almighty led me from my father's house and from the land of my kindred. They came to me and spoke to me. He promised to me saying, I give this land to you and onto your children, onto your children's offspring, onto your children offspring's descendants, onto your posterity onto certain descendants who are of moral quality and onto a Practitioner of righteousness. Therefore, you will get my son a wife from there and the Almighty will send HIS messenger in front of you. If you do not find a woman willing to depart away and journey with you, if you do not find a woman willing to live, prosper, and die according to our way of living, then you will be innocent and clear from this oath with me. Beware, do not take my son back to that land.

The servant put his hand on top of the thigh of his lord Abraham, and he took an oath to Abraham concerning that matter. All the goods of his master Abraham was put under his authority. When he arose, the servant took ten camels from the herd of camels then departed. He went to Aram in Mesopotamia then onto the city of Nahor (**Nah-hore**). At evening time, at the time that women go out to draw water, he made his camels to kneel down outside the city by a well of water. He spoke to the Almighty saying, O Almighty, All Supreme Being, the Ruler of my master Abraham, I pray to you and hope this day You show kindness onto my lord Abraham and send me a good chance of encountering what is appointed to happen. Look and see, I stand here by the water well, and the daughters of the men of the city come out to draw water. Let it come to pass that the young woman I speak to and I ask will you let down your pitcher. I pray that I can drink some water, then she speaks to me saying, drink and I will give your camels a drink also. Let her be the same woman that you have appointed for Your servant Isaac. By this, I will understand that You have shown kindness, mercy and faithfulness onto my lord Abraham. By this, I will know by experience. I will acknowledge and declare you are my master's familiar friend. Before he was done speaking, it came to pass that he looked and Rebekah (**Riv-cah**) came out with her pitcher upon her shoulder. Rebekah (**Riv-kah**) was born to Bethuel (**Beth-thu-ale**). Bethuel is the son of Milcah (**Mil-cah**). Milcah is the adopted daughter of Haran. Milcah is the wife of Nahor. Nahor is Abraham's brother. Rebekah is a virgin and this young woman is very beautiful to look at. She is happy and kind. She has not known any man in any sexual relations. Now, she went down to the well and filled her pitcher. The servant of Abraham ran to meet her and spoke to her saying, I pray you will let me drink a little water from your pitcher.

She answered saying, drink, my lord. Then, she moved quickly with her hands and let down her pitcher to give him a drink of water. When she finished giving him a drink of water, she spoke to him saying, I will draw some water for your camels until they are finished drinking. She moved quickly and emptied her pitcher into the trough, then went back to the well to draw water for all his camels. The servant of Abraham was astonished. He began to gaze and wonder at her yet he held his peace to understand whether the Almighty had made his journey prosperous or not. As the camels finished drinking water, it came to pass, for Rebekah's ears, the servant of Abraham took two golden earrings with the weight of a half shekel, and for her hands he took two bracelets of gold that weighed ten shekels. He spoke to her, asking, whose daughter are you? I pray that you tell me if there is room in your father's house for me to lodge in? She answered him, saying, I am the daughter of Bethuel (**Beth-thu-ale**). Bethuel is the son of Milcah and Nahor. Nahor is Bethuel's father. She continued speaking to him saying, also, we have enough straw for the camels. We have enough provender and room for you to lodge in. In awe and fear, the servant of Abraham humbly bowed down his head to worship the ALMIGHTY. He spoke saying, blessed be the Almighty, the All Supreme Ruler of my lord, Abraham. Praise be to the Almighty who has not left my master empty of His mercy nor His truth. Now, I, living according to the customs and manner of the Almighty have led me to the house of my lord's brethren. Rebekah ran and told them of her mother's house all these things. Rebekah had a brother in law. His name is Laban (**Lah-von**). When Laban saw the earring and bracelets upon his sister's hands, and when he heard the words of his sister Rebekah saying, this is what the servant of Abraham told to me, it came to pass, Laban ran out to the water well to meet the servant of Abraham. Laban came near to the servant of Abraham and the servant stood by the camels at the water well. Laban asked him, why are you standing outside? Come, you are blessed of the Almighty. I have prepared the house you and the room for the camels. The servant went to the house, and he unclothed his camels in their room, then he gave the camels straw and provender. The servant of Abraham was given water to wash his feet and water to wash the men's feet that were with him. Food was set in front of him to eat, but he spoke saying, I will not eat until I have told my message and about my errand. The servant of Abraham was told to speak on. He spoke saying, on all sides, I am Abraham's servant. The Almighty has greatly loved my lord, Abraham. He has blessed my master to be greatly praised and loved, therefore, my lord Abraham has become great and powerful. The Almighty has given him flocks, herds, silver, gold, menservants, maidservants, camels, and asses. In her old age Sarah, my master's wife, gave birth to a son for my lord and onto him my lord Abraham has given all that he has. My lord made me take an oath saying, you will not get my son a woman to wife from the Canaanites. The Canaanites are in the land where my lord lives. But, he said, you will go to my father's house, to my brethren and get a woman for my son to marry. I spoke to my lord asking, what if I do not find a woman willing to depart away and journey with me? What if I do not find a woman willing to live, prosper, and die according to our way of living? My lord answered me saying, I live according to the Covenant of the Almighty, therefore, the Almighty, the All Supreme Being, the All Supreme Ruler will send HIS messenger with me and my journey will prosper.

So, I obeyed my lord, and came here to get a woman of his brethren of his father's house to be a wife for his son. Then, I will be innocent and clear from my oath to him. My lord continued speaking to me saying, when I come to his brethren and they do not give me a woman to be a wife for his son, then I will be innocent and clear of my oath to him. This day, I came to the water well and I spoke saying, O Almighty, All Supreme Ruler of my lord Abraham, now, if You have made my journey to be prosperous, look and see, I stand by the water well. When the appointed virgin comes forth to draw water, and I speak to her saying, I pray you will give me a little water to drink from your pitcher. And she answers me saying I will give you a drink of some water, and I will draw some water for your camels, then let this young woman be the same woman whom the Almighty has appointed for my lord's son. Before I was finished speaking in mine heart, behold, Rebekah came forth with her pitcher on her shoulder. She went down to the well and drew water. I spoke to her saying, I pray you will let me drink some water from your pitcher. She moved quickly, and let down her pitcher from her shoulder. She spoke to me saying, drink some water, and I will give your camels water to drink, so I drank the water and she gave the camels a drink of water also. I asked her, whose daughter are you? She answered saying, I am the daughter of Bethuel. Bethuel is the son of Nahor. Nahor's wife, Milcah gave birth to Bethuel, then I put the earrings upon her ears, and the bracelets upon her hands. Then, I humbly bowed down my head, and worshipped the Almighty as the All Supreme Being, the All Supreme Ruler, the Creator of all things. Indeed, I praised and adored the Almighty, the All Supreme

Ruler of my lord Abraham because He led me in the right way to take my lord's brother's granddaughter to be with his son. Now, if you deal kindly and truly with my lord, tell me. If not, tell me, so I can turn to the right or to the left. Then Laban and Bethuel answered saying, this matter comes forward from the ALMIGHTY. We cannot speak onto you bad or good. Look and see, Rebekah is in front of you, take her, and go. Let her be your lord's son's wife as the Almighty has spoken and commanded. It came to pass that when Abraham's servant heard their words, he worshipped the Almighty by humbly bowing himself to the earth. The servant of Abraham brought forth jewels of silver, jewels of gold, and clothing. He gave them to Rebekah. He gave precious things to her brother and to her mother. Abraham's servant and the men that were with him did eat and drink. They stayed all night and they rose up in the morning. Abraham's servant spoke saying, send me away onto my lord. Rebekah's brother and her mother spoke saying, let the young woman stay with us a few days, at the least ten days then after that she will go. Abraham's servant answered them saying, do not hinder me, do not stop me, seeing the Almighty has caused my journey to prosper. Send me away so I can go to my lord. They answered Abraham's servant saying, we will call the young woman and find out what she has to say. They called Rebekah and spoke to her asking, will you go with this man? Rebekah answered saying, I will go. They sent their sister Rebekah away along with Rebekah's nurse, Abraham's servant, and his men. They blessed Rebekah. They praised and congratulated her. They spoke to her saying, you are our sister and in number you will be the mother of thousands, and they will become millions in number, therefore, for an inheritance, let your children, your children's descendants, and your posterity possess the gates of those that hate them.

Rebekah arose with her young maids, and they rode upon the camels following the servant of Abraham. The servant and Rebekah departed away. Because he lived in southern Mesopotamia, Isaac (**Yitz-hahc**) came to meet them from the way of the Beerlahairoi (**Be-air-lah-hi- ro -ee**) water well. At the evening, Isaac went out into the field to meditate on his possessions and his responsibilities, then he lifted up his eyes, and saw that camels were coming. When she saw Isaac, Rebekah lifted up eyes and she fell down off the camel. Rebekah spoke to the servant of Abraham asking, who is this man that walks in the field to meet us? Abraham's servant answered her saying, it is Isaac, my lord's son. Rebekah took a veil and covered herself. The servant told Isaac all the things that he had done. Isaac brought her into his mother Sarah's tent and had sexual relations with Rebekah, and she became his wife. Isaac loved her as his own family and as a friend. He loved to eat and drink with her. He loved her appetite for wisdom and righteousness. After his mother's death, Isaac repented and found comfort in the Almighty. Then Abraham took another woman to be his wife. Her name was Keturah (**ket-teur-rah**). For Abraham, she gave birth to Zimran (**Zim-ron**), then Jokshan (**Yoke-shawn**), then Medan (**Meh-don**), then Midian (**Mid-dee-yon**). Midian is the progenitor of the Midianites. Keturah gave birth to Ishbak (**Ish-bach**), then Shuah (**Shu-achk**). Jokshan fathered Sheba (**Sheh-vah**) then Dedan (**Dah-don**). The sons of Dedan were Asshurim (**Ash-shur-ree**), then Letushim (**Let-too-shem**), then Leummim (**Leh-oo-meem**). The sons of Midian were Ephah (**Ay-phah**), then Epher (**Ay-fare**), then Hanoch (**Han-no**), then Abida (**Av-vee-dah**), then Eldaah (**ale-dah-ah**). All these were the children of Keturah. But, Abraham gave all that he had to his son Isaac. While he was still living, onto his concubines' sons that Abraham fathered, Abraham gave them gifts, then sent them away from his son Isaac. Abraham sent them eastward onto the east country. Abraham lived to be one hundred eighty-five years old. Then Abraham was brought to his people who were gathered together and Abraham took his last breath, breathed out his soul, and his body died. Abraham full of years and in a good old age. He died an old man. Abraham's sons, Isaac and Ishmael buried him in the field of Ephron (**Ef-roan**) in the cave of Machpelah (**Makh-pay-lah**) that is before Mamre (**Mam-ray**).Ephron is the son of Zohar (**Tso-hair**), the Hittite (**Haith-ee**). Abraham was buried with his wife Sarah in the same field he purchased from the sons of Heth (**Haith**). After the death of Abraham, in came to pass, the ALMIGHTY blessed Abraham's son Isaac. The ALMIGHTY caused him to be praised and adored. Isaac (**Yitz-hoc**) live by the water well Beerlahairoi (**Be-air-lah-hi- ro -ee**). These are the generations of Abraham's son, Ishmael (**Yish-mah-ale**). According to their generations, by their honor, by their glory, by their reputation, and by their authority, the firstborn son of Ishmael is Nebajoth (**Nev-vee-yoth**), then Kedar (**Kay-dar**), then Adbeel (**Ab-bee-ale**), then Mibsam (**Mib-sum**), then, Mishma (**Mish-mah**), then, Dumah (**Dew-mah**), then Massa (**Ma-sah**), then Hadar (**Had-dair**), then Tema (**Tay-mah**), then Jetur (**Yet-teur**), then Naphish (**Nah-pheesh**), and, Kedemah (**Kay-dah-mah**). These are the sons of Ishmael, and these are their names after their towns and after their castles. It was twelve kings according to their gentile nation of people. Ishmael lived to be one hundred thirty-seven years. He was brought to his people who were gathered together. Then he took has last breath of air, breathed out his soul, and died in the presence of all his brethren.

Ishmael's people lived from Havilah (**Hav-vee-lah**) onto Shur (**Sure**). Shur is before Egypt, as you go toward Assyria. Now, these are the generations of Abraham's son, Isaac. Isaac was forty years old when he took Rebekah (**Rev-kah**) to be a wife. Rebekah is the sister of Laban (**Lah-von**), the Syrian (**Air-rah-my**). Rebekah is the daughter of Bethuel (**Beth-thu-ale**). Bethuel is known as the Syrian of Padan-Aram (**Pad-don**). Isaac worshipped the Almighty as the All Supreme Being, as the All Supreme Ruler, as the Creator of all things and because Isaac's wife was sterile, Isaac prayed with a plea to the Almighty. Because Isaac prayed and worshiped the Almighty, Isaac's wife Rebekah conceived, indeed, she became pregnant. Within her, two male children struggled together as one trying to crush the other as one trying to oppress the other. She spoke to herself asking, if this is right, why is it like this within me? Rebekah did not resort to a person nor did she resort to a god of necromancy. Rebekah did not seek out any deity with prayer and worship. Rebekah had gone to worship the Almighty, the All Supreme Being, the All Supreme Ruler, the Creator of all things. Carefully, she sought the Almighty with worship and prayer. The Almighty spoke to her and declared to her saying, two different nations of people are in your womb. Two different manners of people, with different judgments, different actions, and different truths will be separated from your womb. The older son and his seed will be stone-hearted. They will prove to be stronger in body, and stronger in courage, therefore, the older son and his seed will be stronger than the younger son and his seed, but on all sides, the seed of your eldest son will be made to serve and remain serving the seed of your younger son.

They seed of your younger son will be of the service to honor the Almighty. When her time was fulfilled and she was ready to deliver, there were twins in her womb. The firstborn came out a dark reddish color with rough hair like an animal. The rough hair covered him like a garment of fur. Rebekah and Isaac called his name Esau (**Eh-sav**). Right after that, his brother came out, and his hand had taken hold onto Esau's heel. His name was called Jacob (**Yah-cove**). Isaac was sixty years old when Rebekah gave birth to them. The boys grew in body, mind, and honor. Esau was an experienced hunter. He was a wild man of the open country. He was a man of the wilderness. Jacob was a completely upright man. He was undefiled. He was morally innocent, ethically pure, and having integrity. He was quiet and gentle. He did not lack beauty. He did not lack physical strength. He lived in tents. Isaac loved Esau as his own family and as his friend. Isaac loved to eat the food Esau hunted. Together, they would eat, drink, and share wisdom. Rebekah loved Jacob as her own family and as her friend. Together, they would eat, drink, and share wisdom. Esau came from the wilderness of the open country and he was thirsty and exhausted. In his heart, Jacob was angry with the Almighty, but he did not express his feelings. As Jacob was seething, he was boiling a dark red soup. Esau, arrogant, and proud against the Almighty, spoke to Jacob saying, I pray that you will feed me with that same bloody soup of water, lentils, and cow. Jacob responded saying, this day sell me your birthright. Surrender your birthright to me. Sell me your right of being the firstborn. Esau answered, saying, look and see, I am at the point of being a dead man. What profit will my birthright do for me? What profit will my right of being the firstborn do for me? Jacob answered saying, this day, take an oath to me. Esau took an oath to Jacob and sold his birthright to Jacob. Jacob gave Esau bread and boiled soup of lentils and cow.

Esau did eat and drink, then rose up and went his way to live and die according to his own manner. Because of this, Esau regarded his right of being the firstborn as despicable and worthless. Esau despised his birthright. Beside the first famine of hunger that was in the days of Abraham (**Av-rah-hum**), there was a famine of hunger in the land. Then, the Almighty considered and gave His attention to Isaac. As the Almighty had foreseen, HE appeared to Isaac in a vision. The Almighty was visible to Isaac, and the Almighty spoke to him, commanding him, saying, do not go into Egypt, but live in the land that I tell you to. Live and travel in this land and I will be with you. I will bless you to be praised and adored. To you, it is ordained and appointed. I will give you all the nations and countries in the land. I will give this land to the children of your semen, to the offspring of their children, to their descendants, to the offspring of their descendants, and to their posterity. Of your posterity, I will give this land to those descendants of moral quality and to a practitioner of My righteousness. I will perform the oath that I promised your father Abraham. I will make descendants of your children multiply to be great in number. In the land of the living, to the ends of the Earth, I will make the descendants of your posterity to be as numerous as the stars in heaven. All nations of the Earth joined to them will be blessed. This will come to pass because your father Abraham paid attention to Me. This will come to pass because he listened to Me with interest and obeyed My voice. This will happen because he observed and preserved My Covenant and My Law. With interest, Isaac paid attention to the Almighty. He listened with interest and obeyed the Almighty, the All Supreme Being, the All

Supreme Ruler. Isaac did not go to Egypt. Isaac (**Yitz-hoc**) went to Gerar (**Geh-rar**) to meet Abimelech (**Av-vee-mel-lek**) king of the Philistines (**Pel-lesh-tee**). So, Isaac lived in Gerar. The men of the place asked Isaac about his wife. Isaac feared to tell them that she was his wife unless, as he thought, the men of the place would kill him to take possession of his wife Rebekah. She is very beautiful and of a goodly form that is pleasant to look upon. Isaac answered saying, she is my sister. When Isaac had been there a long time Abimelech, king of the Philistines, looked out of a window and saw Isaac. Isaac was being merry, laughing, and playing with Rebekah. Abimelech called to Isaac and spoke to him, saying, the woman is certainly your wife. Why did you tell me she is your sister? Isaac responded to him saying, I thought I would be killed for her. I thought a warlock magician of necromancy would put me to death to take her for a possession. Abimelech responded asking, what is this you have done to us? One of the people might have soon relaxed with your wife and laid down with her in sexual relations, then you would have brought sin and guiltiness upon us. Abimelech set up orders and commanded all his people saying, he that touches Isaac or his wife will surely be put to death. Then Isaac sowed in that land by scattering seeds, then in the same year, he received one hundred fold for every seed he scattered. He received a one hundred fold blessing. The Almighty, the All Supreme Being, the All Supreme Ruler, the Creator of all things blessed Isaac. The Almighty caused Isaac to be praised and adored. Isaac was a steward of mankind. He was a servant of the Almighty. He lived and talked according to the manner of the Almighty and he lived to die in the ways of the Almighty. Isaac grew in importance. He did great things. The Almighty made him become powerful, and Isaac became a man of high degree. Isaac grew until he became very great. He had possession of flocks, possession of herds, and a great multitude of servants.

The Philistines became very jealous and angry. They closed their eyes at him and they envied him. From the days of Abraham, all the water wells that Abraham's servants dug, the Philistines filled them with earth and stopped them. Abimelech spoke to Isaac, commanding him saying, you go away from us because you have greatly increased in number, because you are more powerful and much mightier than we are. Isaac departed away from there. He pitched his tent in the valley of Gerar and lived there. Isaac dug the wells of water again. The same water wells that were dug in the days of Abraham by his servants. Isaac called the names of these wells after the names that his father called them. Isaac's servants were digging in the valley and found water for a well. With words, the herd men of Gerar (**Geh-rar**) argued and complained against Isaac's herd men saying, this water is ours. Physically the herd men of Gerar did contend against the herd men of Isaac. Therefore, Isaac called the name of the well Esek (**Ay-sek**) the well of contention because the herd men of Gerar quarreled with him. Isaac dug another water well, and they contended for that also. Isaac called the name of the water well Sitnah (**Sit-nah**), a well of strife, because the herd men of Gerar quarreled with him. Isaac removed his tent from there and left away to another part of the valley. He dug another water well and there was no contention, no strife, no quarrel. Isaac called the name of it Rehoboth (**Reh-ho-voath**), a water well in wide places. Now, Isaac spoke to himself saying, the Almighty has made room for us, and we will be fruitful in this land. From there, Isaac went to Beersheba (**Bah-air-sheh-bah**). There, Abimelech responded to Isaac, saying, we saw and it has been revealed to us that the Almighty is certainly with you.

Now, I declare there be an oath between you and us, even between us and you. Let us make a covenant, a friendship, and alliance with you. As we have not touched you, as we have done nothing to you but good. We have sent you away in peace, now you are blessed and adored by the Almighty, therefore, you will do us no harm. Isaac prepared a feast for them, and they did eat and drink. To get an early start, they rose up in the morning, and took an oath one to another. Isaac sent them away, and they departed away from him in peace. The same day, it came to pass, Isaac's servants came and told him about the water well they had dug. They said to him, we have found water. Isaac chose and invited guest to preach to. Isaac preached to them about the Almighty, and called the name of the well Shebah (**Sheh-vah**), a water well of an oath, and the city near to it is Beersheba onto this day. Now, Esau was forty years old when he took possession of a woman for a wife. He married Judith (**Yeh-whoo-deeth**). She was a Canaanitess. She was the daughter of Beeri (**Bay-ay-ree**), the Hittite (Haith), and Bashemath (**Boes-math**), the daughter of Elon (Ay-lone) the Hittite. From their own bitterness, Esau and Judith were saddening the hearts of Isaac and Rebekah. From their own bitterness, Esau and Judith were troubling the minds of Isaac and Rebekah. From their own bitterness, Esau and Judith were grieving the souls of Isaac and Rebekah. When Isaac became older, light was restrained from his eye and his vision became very dim. He called to his eldest son Esau and spoke to him saying, my son. Esau responded saying, I am here. Isaac spoke to Esau saying, look and see. I am older and I do not know the day of my death. Now, I pray that you take possession of your weapons, your quiver and your bow, then go out into the field to hunt and catch some food for me. Prepare tasty meat for me. Prepare the food with the taste I love, and I will eat and drink.

Bring it to me so I can eat and I will congratulate you. I praise and adore you. I will bless you before I die. While Isaac was speaking to his son Esau, Rebekah listened with interest. She heard and understood what Isaac was saying to Esau. Esau departed away and went to the field to hunt and catch some food so he can bring it to his father. Rebekah spoke to her son Jacob saying, I listened and heard your father speaking to your brother. He told your brother to bring him some food. Your father commanded your brother to prepare a tasty meat so he can eat, then your father will congratulate him. He will praise and adore him, and he will bless him to be before the Almighty. Now, my son, obey my voice according to what I command you to do. Go to the flock, and get me two good kids of the goats. I will prepare them and make them to be a tasty meat for your father just as he loves. You will bring it to your father so he can eat. Then he can congratulate you. He will praise and adore you. He will bless you to be before the Almighty before his death. Jacob responded to his mother Rebekah, saying, my brother Esau is a rough and hairy man, but I am a smooth man. What if my father touches me then I will seem to him a mocker, a cheat, a deceiver. I will bring a bitter curse upon me and not a blessing. Jacob's mother answered him, saying, my son, your curse be upon me, only obey my voice and go get me two good kid goats from the flock. Jacob went and got two good kids of the goats. He brought them to his mother. His mother made a tasty meat just as Isaac loved. From their house, Rebekah took goodly garments that belonged to her eldest son Esau. She put them upon her younger son Jacob. She put the skin of the goats upon his hands, and upon his smooth neck. She put the tasty meat and the bread she prepared into the hand of Jacob. Jacob went to his father and spoke to him saying, my father. Isaac answered saying, I am here, who are you my son? Jacob spoke to his father saying, I am Esau, your firstborn. I have done according to your command. Now, arise. I pray that you sit and eat the food I caught then you can bless me. Isaac spoke to his son asking, how is it that you have found it so quickly? Jacob responded saying, the Almighty brought it to me. Isaac spoke to Jacob saying, my son, come near. I pray you will so I can touch you. I want to feel you to tell whether you are my son Esau or not. Jacob went near to his father Isaac, and Isaac felt him. Isaac spoke saying, the voice is Jacob's voice, but the hands are the hands of Esau. Isaac spoke to Jacob asking, are you my son Esau? Jacob responded saying, I am. Isaac continued speaking to Jacob saying, bring the food near me, and I will eat my son's food he hunted and caught from the field, then my soul will bless you. Jacob brought the food near him, and Isaac did eat. Jacob brought him wine, and Isaac did drink. Isaac spoke to Jacob saying, now come near me. Kiss me, my son. Jacob came near and kissed his father Isaac. Isaac smelled the fragrance of Jacob's clothing, then blessed him. Isaac spoke to himself saying, the smell of my son is as the fragrance of a field that the Almighty has blessed. Isaac did not discern nor did he distinguish Jacob from Esau because as Esau's hands were rough and hairy, so was Jacob's hands. Isaac congratulated Jacob. Isaac blessed him to be praised and adored. Isaac blessed Jacob saying, as dew from heaven covers the vegetation, the Almighty will give you plenty in great abundance. The Almighty will give you strong men, richly prepared food, and the fertile places of the Earth. The Almighty will give you plenty of corn and wine. The people will serve you, and nations will bow down to you.

You will be lord over your brethren, and your mother's sons will bow down to you. Everyone that despises you, everyone that curses you, everyone that treats you with little worth, will themselves be despised, will themselves be bitterly cursed, will themselves be treated with little worth. Everyone that blesses you, everyone that congratulates and praises you, everyone that adores you, will themselves be blessed, will themselves be congratulated, will themselves be praised, will themselves be adored. As soon as Isaac had made an end of blessing Jacob, it came to pass, as Jacob had not yet gone far away from the presence of his father Isaac, Esau came back from his hunting. Esau also made tasty meat, and brought it to his father. Esau spoke to his father saying, let my father arise, and eat of his son's food so your soul can bless me. Isaac spoke to Esau asking, who are you? Esau responded saying, I am your son, Esau, I am your firstborn. Isaac was startled and very discomfited. He began trembling and moving about. Isaac responded to Esau asking him, who? Where is the man that has taken hold of some hunted food and brought it to me? Before you came, I ate all that was in front of me and blessed him. Yes. Indeed. He will be blessed. He will be congratulated, praised, and adored. When Esau heard the words of his father, he understood. He wept with a very great cry and spoke to his father Isaac saying, father, bless me also. Isaac responded saying, your brother was treacherous. He came to me and used a deceitful craft. Therefore, he has taken away your blessing. Esau responded to Isaac saying, without a doubt, he is rightly named Jacob because he has taken hold of my heel and held me back two times. He took possession of my birthright as the firstborn. Now, look and see. In my blessing, he has replaced me with himself, then he took possession of my blessing. He has taken possession of both my blessings. Have you not reserved a blessing for me? Isaac answered Esau saying, I have set him to be a sign. I have ordained and appointed him to be your lord. I have given all his brethren to him for servants. I have sustained him with corn and wine. Now, my son, what will I do onto you? Esau spoke to his father, asking, have you only one blessing? Father, bless me then bless me again, then Esau lifted up his voice and wept. Isaac answered Esau saying, look and see. As dew from heaven covers the vegetation, the Almighty will give you plenty in great abundance. The Almighty will give you strong men, richly prepared food, and the fertile places of the Earth. When you have mourned and wandered restlessly, it will come to pass, you will break your brother's yoke from off your neck, you will be ruler and you will have the dominion. You will live and sustain yourself by your sword, and on all sides, you will serve your brother, who is a worshipper of the Almighty. Esau hated Jacob because of the blessing that his father blessed him with. Esau retained his animosity for Jacob and cherished the hate he had for his brother Jacob. Speaking to himself, Esau said, when the days of mourning my father is at an end, then I will lurk, lay snares, and kill my brother Jacob. Esau's words were told to his mother Rebekah. She sent for her young son Jacob. She spoke to him saying, look and see. Your older brother Esau, will comfort himself by killing you. Esau is purposing to put you to death. Now, my son, obey my voice and arise. You run and escape to my brother Laban (**Lah-von**) who is in Haran (**Chah-run**). Until your brother's fury and anger is removed, stay and live with Laban for a little time. Why should I lose both my children in one day?

Until your brother's anger is turned away from you and he forgets what you have done to him, stay and live with Laban. Then, I will send someone to come and get you from there. Rebekah spoke to Isaac, saying, I am exhausted and weary of my life because of the daughters of Heth (**Haith**). If Jacob takes a woman to be a wife from the daughters of Heth, or any woman that is like the daughters of Canaan, to what good will my life be to me? Isaac called for Jacob to preach to him. Isaac proclaimed the authority, the reputation, the honor, the character, and the glory of the Almighty, the All Supreme Being, the All Supreme Ruler, the Creator of all things. Isaac congratulated and praised Jacob. Isaac charged him with the Commandment that comes from the Almighty. Then, Isaac spoke to Jacob saying, you will not take possession of a woman to be a wife from the daughters of Canaan (**Ken-ah-an**). Now, arise, go to Padan (**Pad-don**), to the house of Bethuel. Bethuel is your mother's father. From there, from the daughters your mother's brother Laban, take possession of a woman to be a wife. The Almighty will bless you. HE will cause you to be congratulated, praised, and adored. He will make you fruitful. HE will multiply you so you can be a multitude of people. The Almighty will give you the blessing of your grandfather Abraham and to your children and to your children's offspring and to their offspring's descendants, to your posterity and of your posterity, to descendants of moral quality and of them, to a practitioner of the Almighty's righteousness. You will inherit this land that the Almighty gave to Abraham where now you are a stranger in. Then, Isaac sent Jacob away. Jacob went to Laban in Padan. Laban is the brother of Rebekah and the son of Bethuel, the

Syrian (**Air-rah-my**). Esau watched his father Isaac as he bless his brother Jacob. Esau saw his father and brother look at one another with joy and respect. Esau watched his father command Jacob to go to Padan to take a woman to be a wife. Esau understood when Isaac told Jacob that he will not take a woman to be a wife from the daughters of Canaan. Esau saw that Jacob obeyed his father and his mother. He saw Jacob leave to go to Padan. Esau considered. He gave his attention to this and discerned. Then, it was revealed onto him that the daughters of Canaan displeased his father Isaac and his mother Rebekah. Then Esau went to Ishmael (**Yish-mah-ale**) and took possession of women to be wives. One of the women Esau married was Mahalath (**Makh-al-lath**). Mahalath is a daughter of Ishmael. Mahalath is the sister of Nebjoth (**Nev-vee-ath**). Nebjothm is the progenitor of the Nabateans and a son of Ishmael. Ishmael is Abraham's son. Jacob departed away from Beersheba (**Bay-air-sheh-bah**) and went toward Haran. Unaware, Jacob's journey had reached to the border of a certain place. Because the sun was setting, he decided to stay there the course of the night. Jacob took some stones of that place and used them for pillows, then he laid down in that place to sleep. He began to dream and he beheld the Earth and a staircase that went upward like a ladder. The tip top of it reached to the atmosphere of the sky where the clouds move. A king, angels, officers, deputies, messengers, priests, prophets, and teachers of the Eloheem were ascending and descending on it. They built this staircase to stand firm, then they took their stand. They struck at the heaven of the Almighty. They reached up to put their strength and power in the heaven of the Almighty. They reached up to take away the heaven of the Almighty by violence. Beyond their control by fate, they were punished, plagued with disease, defeated, destroyed, and the staircase was brought down. Jacob looked and beheld.

Above all them, the Almighty, the All Supreme Being, the All Supreme Ruler, the Creator of all things was set up and established. The Almighty was standing above them, and He spoke to Jacob, saying, I am the ALMIGHTY, the ALL SUPREME BEING, the ALL SUPREME RULER, the CREATOR of all things, I am the ALL SUPREME RULER of your grandfather Abraham. I am the ALL SUPREME RULER of your father Isaac. I will give you the land you are resting on. I will give it to your children, to your children's offspring, to your children's offsprings' descendants, onto your posterity, and of your posterity, onto descendants of moral quality, and of those descendants, onto a practitioner of My righteousness. Then, in number, your descendants will become as the dust of the earth. I will spread them abroad to the west, to east, to the north, and to the south. All the families of the Earth that are joined to you will be blessed. All the families of the Earth joined to those descendants of moral quality will be blessed. The Almighty continued speaking to Jacob saying, I am with you. I am your keeper. Beware, you are treasured in my memory. I will observe you and watch over you. I will protect you and save your life. I will keep My Covenant with you, I will observe it with you, and I will perform My vow. You will be restrained because I will keep you within the bounds of My Covenant. Wherever you go, I will observe you. I will watch over you. I will protect you and save your life. I will bring you back into this land again. I will not leave you nor your children, nor your children's offspring, nor your children's offsprings' descendants, nor your posterity, nor of your posterity, those descendants of moral quality, nor of those descendants, the practitioner of MY righteousness until I have performed and finished what I have spoken to you of. Jacob awoke from his sleep and became active. He spoke to himself saying, surely the Almighty, the All Supreme Being, the All Supreme Ruler is in this place. This was not revealed to me. I did not consider because I did not know. Standing in awe, Jacob became afraid. He was astonished and fearful. He repented and became afraid to do terrible things. He was inspired to honor and respect the Almighty. Jacob spoke to himself saying, the place of the Eloheem's heaven is dreadful and terrifying. That was the house and the affairs of the Eloheem, and this is the gate entrance to reach their city, marketplaces, and palaces. Jacob rose up early in the morning. He took the stones that he had used for pillows and used them to set up a pillar for a memorial. He poured oil upon the top of this memorial. Jacob made a vow, and he promised, saying, if the Almighty be with me and if He protects me on this journey that I go, if the Almighty will provide me with food to eat and clothing to put on so I can come again to my father's house in peace, then the Almighty, the All Supreme Being, the Creator of all things will be my All Supreme Ruler. These stones that I have set up for a memorial will be to honor the house of the Almighty. Jacob chose and invited guests to preach to. Then, he proclaimed the honor, the reputation, the authority, the character, and the glory of the Almighty, the All Supreme Being, the All Supreme Ruler, the Creator of all things. Jacob named that place (**Bah-yith Shah-dye**), the house of the Almighty, but at first, the name of that city was called Luz (**Looz**). Then Jacob departed away from there and continued on his journey. He came into the land of the people of the east. He considered and observed. He looked and saw a water well in the field. There were three flocks of sheep resting by it. Out of this water well, the people gave water to their flocks and a great stone covered the well's opening.

There, when all the flocks were gathered, they rolled the stone away from the well's opening, then they gave water to the sheep and put the stone back in its place over the well's opening. Jacob spoke to the people asking, where are you from, my brethren? They answered saying, we are of Haran (**Hah-run**). Jacob responded asking, do you know Laban, the son of Nahor? They answered saying, yes, we know him. Jacob responded asking, is he doing well? They answered saying, yes, he is doing well. His daughter Rachel (**Rah-hail**) is coming with their sheep. Jacob responded saying, it is not yet the highest point of the day, neither is it time for the cattle to be gathered together. Go, you can give water to the sheep and feed them. The people replied to Jacob saying, we cannot until all the flocks are assembled and gathered together. We cannot until they roll the stone from off the opening of the water well. While Jacob was still speaking with them, Rachel came with her father's flock of sheep. Rachel observed and watched over her father's sheep. She cared for them and protected them. Rachel was the daughter of Laban (**Lah-von**). Laban is Jacob's mother's brother. When Jacob saw Rachel with her father's sheep, he went near the stone that was covering the opening of the water well, then he rolled the stone from off the opening of the water well. Now, Laban had men equipped with weapons under his rule. These men were equipped to handle other armed men. Jacob also had armed men under his rule. Jacob was armed with a weapon and he also was equipped to handle armed men. Then, Jacob started giving water to the sheep of Laban. Laban is Jacob's mother's brother. Among the men armed with weapons who were equipped to handle other armed men, Jacob spoke to Rachel gently touched her and kissed her. Then, Jacob lifted-up his voice and began to weep. Jacob told Rachel that he is Rebekah's son, and Rebekah is her father's brother. Then, Rebekah ran and told her father Laban. When Laban listened to the announcement about his sister's son Jacob, Laban ran to meet him. Laban embraced Jacob with his arms and hands and gently kissed him, then brought him to his house. Jacob told Laban all these things that happened. Laban spoke to Jacob saying, surely, you are of the same strength as my flesh and bones. Surely you are my brethren. When Jacob had lived with him a period of one month, Laban spoke to Jacob saying, because you are my brother, should you serve me for nothing? Tell me what your wages will be. Laban had two daughters. The name of the elder was Leah (**Lay-ah**), and the name of the younger was Rachel (Rah-hail). Leah had a soft heart and a gentle spirit. She was timid and delicate. She spoke soft and gentle words. Rachel was very beautiful. She was of a beautiful figure and of a beautiful appearance. Rachel was well favored. Jacob loved Rachel as his own family and as a friend. He loved to eat and drink with her. He loved to share wisdom with her. Jacob greatly desired her. Jacob spoke to Rachel's father Laban saying, I am a servant of the Almighty, the All Supreme Being, the All Supreme Ruler, now for your younger daughter Rachel, I will serve you seven years. Laban responded to Jacob, saying, it is better I give her to you than give her to another man. Therefore, you stay with me. For Rachel, Jacob, a servant of the Almighty served Laban seven years. Because of the love Jacob had for Rachel, the time he served her father Laban seemed but as a few days to him. When his days of service were fulfilled, Jacob spoke to Laban saying, give me my wife so I can show my affections to her so I can go in to know her as my wife. Laban gathered all the men of the place together because he had prepared a feast.

In the night, it came to pass, Laban took his daughter Leah to give to Jacob. For a handmaid, Laban had given his daughter Leah his maid Zilpah (**Zil-pah**). Jacob went in onto her to show her affections and know her as his wife. In the morning, Jacob looked and saw he was with Leah. Therefore, he spoke to Laban asking, what is this that you have done to me? I am a servant and worshipper of the ALMIGHTY, the ALL SUPREME BEING, the ALL SUPREME RULER, did I not serve you for Rachel? Why have you betray me? Why have you deceived me? Laban answered Jacob saying, in our country, to give you the younger daughter before the firstborn daughter is something that must not be done. You have fulfilled seven years of service to have Leah. Now, for another seven years of service, you servant and worshipper of the Almighty, I will give you my younger daughter Rachel, but you will serve me another seven years, and Jacob did so. Then, after seven years, Laban gave Jacob his daughter Rachel to be a wife also. Jacob went in onto Rachel with affection and to know her as his wife. To Rachel, Laban had given Bilhah (**Bil-hah**) to be her handmaid. Jacob loved Rachel more than Leah and Jacob served Laban another seven years. When the Almighty saw that Leah was not loved as Rachel, the Almighty opened her womb to bring forth children, but Rachel's womb remained sterile. Leah became pregnant with a child and gave birth to a son. She spoke to herself saying, now my husband will love me. She chose and invited guests. She preached about the Almighty. She spoke to the guests saying, the Almighty has considered me and observed me. He has seen my affliction. She brought her son before them and called his name Reuben (**Reh-oo-vain**). Leah became pregnant again and gave birth to a second son. She spoke to herself saying, the Almighty knew I have been hated. She chose and invited guests. She preached about the Almighty. She spoke to the guests saying, the Almighty has listened to me. He has paid attention to me. She brought her son before them, and called his name Simeon (**Shem-own**). Leah became pregnant again and gave birth to another son. She spoke to herself saying, because I have given birth to three sons for him, my husband will be united with me. She chose and invited guests. She preached about the Almighty. She brought her son before them, and called his name Levi (**Leh-vee**). Leah became pregnant again and she gave birth to a fourth son. She chose and invited guests. She preached about the Almighty saying, I will praise the Almighty, the All Supreme Being, the All Supreme Ruler, the Creator of all things. She brought her son before them, and called his name Judah (**Yeh-who-dah**). After giving birth to four sons, Leah stopped having children. Now, Rachel believed she could not give to birth to children for Jacob, so she became very jealous of her sister Leah. When Rachel's jealousy escalated to a jealous anger, she spoke to her husband Jacob saying, give me children or else I will prematurely die. From longsuffering, Jacob began to be angry at Rachel. He spoke to her saying, am I in the place of the Almighty. It is HE that has restrained your womb. Rachel responded saying, look. Bilhah, my maid, you go in with affections to her and know her as your wife. She will give birth to children for me so I will have children by her. Rachel gave her handmaid Bilhah to Jacob to be a wife. Jacob went in with affections to her. Bilhah became pregnant and she gave birth to a son for Jacob. Rachel spoke to herself saying, the Almighty has judged me and He has executed His judgment. Rachel chose and invited guests. She preached about the Almighty saying, the Almighty has considered me and my trouble.

The Almighty has heard my voice, therefore, He has given me a son. Rachel brought her son before them, and called the boy's name Dan (**Don**). Bilhah, Rachel's handmaid, became pregnant again and gave birth to a second son for Jacob. Rachel spoke to herself saying, I have bitterly struggled with my sister. Now I have power to overcome. Rachel chose and invited guests. She spoke to them saying, I have had many great struggles. Now I have the strength to overcome. I am able to accomplish and endure. She brought the boy before the guests and called his name Naphtali (**Naph-tah-lee**). Now, Leah believed she could no longer give birth to children so she took her handmaid Zilpah and gave her to Jacob to be a wife. Zilpah, Leah's handmaid, gave birth to a son for Jacob. Leah spoke to herself saying, good fortune comes. Leah named the boy Gad (**God**). Zilpah, Leah's handmaid, gave birth to a second son for Jacob. Leah spoke to herself saying, now I am happy. The daughters of the town will call me blessed. Leah named the boy Asher (**Ah-share**). During the days of the wheat harvest, Reuben went out and found herbs and apples in the field. He brought them to his mother Leah. Rachel asked Leah, will you give me some of your son's apples? Leah spoke to Rachel saying, is it a small matter that you have taken my husband? Now, would you take away my son's apples also? Leah continued speaking to Rachel saying, for my son's apples, Jacob will lie with me tonight. In the evening, Jacob came from the field. Leah went out to meet him and said, you must come in and lay with me. I have paid for you with my son's apples. Jacob laid in affection with Leah that night. With interest, the Almighty listened to Leah's voice. HE understood her case and obeyed the request of her plea.

Leah became pregnant and gave birth to a fifth son for Jacob. Leah spoke to herself saying, because I have given my handmaid to my husband, the Almighty has given me my reward. Leah called the boy's name Issachar (**Yis-hah-har**). Leah became pregnant again and she gave birth to a sixth son for Jacob. She spoke to herself saying, because I have given him six sons, my husband will live with me. Leah chose and invited guests. She preached about the Almighty. She spoke to them saying, the Almighty has bestowed a precious gift upon me. He has bestowed endurance upon me. She brought her son before them and called his name Zebulun (**Zev-voo-loon**). Afterwards, Leah gave birth to a daughter. She called her girl's name Dinah (**Dee-nah**). The Almighty kept Rachel in His remembrance. He thought well upon her. Therefore, the Almighty, the All Supreme Being, the All Supreme Ruler, the Creator of all things remembered Rachel. With interest, the Almighty listened to Rachel's voice. He understood her case and obeyed the request of her plea. The Almighty opened her womb so she could give birth to children. Rachel became pregnant and gave birth to a son. She chose and invited guests. She preached about the Almighty saying, the Almighty has taken away my disgrace. He has removed my shame. The Almighty has added another son to me. Rachel brought her son before them and called his name Joseph (**Yo-safe**). When Rachel had given birth to Joseph, Jacob spoke to Laban saying, send me away so I can go back to my country, to my own place. Give me my wives and my children because I have served you for them. Let me go. You know all the service that I have accomplished and completed for you. Laban responded saying, if I have found favor in your eyes, I pray that you stay. I have learned by experience that the Almighty has blessed me for your sake. Laban continued speaking to Jacob saying, you appoint your wages and I will give it. Jacob responded saying, on all sides, you know how I serve and worship the Almighty.

You know how I have served you, and you know how your cattle are with me. You had a little before I came. Now, it has increased to be a multitude. Since my coming, the Almighty has blessed you. Now, when will I provide for my own affairs, when will I provide for my own house? Laban responded to Jacob asking, what can I give you? Jacob answered saying, you will not give me anything. I will keep your flock and feed them again if you will do this thing for me. Today, I will pass through all your flock removing all the speckled and spotted cattle from among the flock. I will be removing all the brown sheep and those brown with some white spot that are among the sheep. I will be removing the spotted and speckled goats from among the flock of goats. These are my wages. In the time to come, my righteousness will answer for me. When my wages come before your face, everyone that is not speckled and spotted among the goats and everyone that is not brown among the sheep with me will be counted stolen. Laban replied saying, I will see to it so it will be according to your word. Jacob took the male goats that were speckled and spotted. All the female goats that were speckled and spotted. All the brown sheep and every one of those brown with some white among the sheep. Jacob listened with interest to the words of Laban's sons. He heard them saying, Jacob has taken away all that belonged to our father. He has taken away everything that has gotten our father his wealth, honor, and glory. Once in the presence of Laban, Jacob looked at Laban. He saw anger on Laban's face. Laban's favor was not toward Jacob as before. The Almighty visited Jacob and spoke to him and commanded him saying, return to the land of your fathers. I will be with you. Jacob called for Rachel and Leah to come to the field to his flock. Jacob spoke to both his wives saying, you know with all my ability, all my strength, and all my wealth; I serve and worship the Almighty, the All Supreme Being, the All Supreme Ruler. You know I have served your father with all my power also. But, your father has mocked me, and he has deceitfully dealt with me. He has changed my wages ten times, but the Almighty has allowed him not to hurt me. I see your father's countenance. He is angry against me. His favor is not toward me as before, but the ALMIGHTY, the ALL SUPREME RULER of my father is with me. If Laban tells me that the speckled of the herd will be my wages, then all the cattle gave birth to speckled cattle. If Laban tells me that the ring striped will be my wages, then all the cattle give birth to ring-striped. Therefore, the Almighty has taken away the cattle from your father and given them to me. At the time the cattle became pregnant, the leader of the people increased the work. He raised a levy and increased it. I had a dream and in this dream, I lifted up my eyes and I saw cattle. Those that were ring striped, speckled, and spotted were superior and excelled. The leaders of the people stirred themselves up and arose to cut off the increase of those cattle. In the dream, the Almighty spoke to me saying, I am the ALMIGHTY, the ALL SUPREME RULER of **Shah-dye Bayith**, where you anointed the pillar of stones? Where you promised and vowed to ME? I have seen all that Laban has done to you. Now, arise, you get from off this land. Return to the land of your fathers. Rachel and Leah responded to Jacob asking, is there any portion of inheritance for us in our father's house? He sold us then consumed and wasted our money also. Are we not counted to him as strangers? All the riches that the Almighty has taken away from our father and given to you is now ours and our children. Whatever the Almighty has commanded of you, you do it. Jacob rose up, then put his sons and wives upon camels.

To go to his father in the land of Canaan, Jacob carried away all his cattle and all his goods that he had gotten. While Laban had gone to shear his sheep, Rachel stole Laban's family's idols of worship. It was cultic objects with the image of gods that was used to worship an idolatrous healer. In secret, Jacob carried everything he had away from Laban the Syrian. Jacob did not tell Laban he had departed away. Jacob departed away with all that had and passed over the river. Jacob set his face toward the mountain of Gilead (**Gil-odd**). On the third day, it was told to Laban that Jacob had departed away. Laban took his brethren with him and eagerly pursued after Jacob a seven days journey. They pursued Jacob hard until the caught up with him. In the night, in a dream the Almighty, the All Supreme Being, the All Supreme Ruler visited Laban the Syrian. In a dream, the Almighty spoke to him warning him saying, beware, save yourself. Beware of the watchman that keeps My Covenant and keeps My Commandments. Beware that you do not speak to Jacob about the good of your prosperity nor the goodness of your wealth. Do not speak to him about your good morals nor about your good ethics. Do not distress him. Do not promise adversity nor mischief to him. Do not speak evilly to him. Treasure this in your memory. Now, Jacob had pitched his tent in the mountain of Gilead. Laban and his brethren also pitched a tent in the mountain of Gilead. Then Laban overtook Jacob. Laban spoke to Jacob saying, what have I done that made you carry off what I am not aware of? What have I done that made you carry away my daughters just as captives are taken with the sword? Why did you depart away secretly and deceive me? You did not tell me so I could not send you away with a festival of joy and gladness, with songs from the tambourine (**Toph**), and from the harp. Why did you not allow me to kiss my grandsons and daughters? Now, you have acted foolishly by doing this? It is in the power of my hand to hurt you and harm you, but the Almighty, the All Supreme Ruler of your father spoke to me last night saying, beware, save yourself. Do not declare to Jacob good things or bad things. I know you want to be gone. You very much want to be at your father's house, but why have you stolen my family idols. Why have you carried off my family's gods? Jacob responded to Laban saying, I was in fear and afraid. I said to myself that you would take my daughters and my wives from me by force. Whoever you search and find your Eloheem with, let him not live. In front of our brethren, you discern and distinguish what is yours that I have with me, then take it into your possession. Jacob did not know his wife Rachel had stolen Laban's gods and angels of worship. Laban went into Jacob's tent, then into Leah's tent. When Laban left out of Leah's tent, he entered into Rachel's tent. Now, Rachel had possession of Laban's family idols. She put them in the camel's furniture and sat on top of them. Laban searched all her tent but did not find them. Rachel spoke to her father, saying, I cannot rise up before you because the custom of women is upon me. I cannot rise up before you, let this not displease my father. Laban continued searching but did not find his family idols. Laban left out of Rachel's tent, then went into the two handmaids' tents, but he did not find them. Jacob became angry. Displeased, he began to grow furious. With words, Jacob began to complain and argue with Laban. Jacob spoke to Laban asking, what is my trespass? What is my sin that has made you hotly pursue after me. Now, you have searched all my stuff. Out of all my household possessions, what have you found?

et it here, in front of my brethren and your brethren and they can judge between both of us. I have been with you these past twenty one years. Your female sheep and your she goats have not miscarried their young. I have not eaten the rams of your flock. I did not bring you the sheep nor the goats that were torn and killed by beasts. Whether they were stolen by day or by night, you required it out of my hand, therefore, I took the loss for it. In the days of parching heat that devoured me, I was under this authority. I was in the frost by night under this authority. No sleep came to my eyes. In your house, I have been under this authority for twenty one years. For fourteen years, I served you for your two daughters and seven years for your cattle. You have changed my wages ten times. Now, surely you would have sent me away empty handed except the Almighty, the All Supreme Ruler of my grandfather Abraham has been with me. Now, surely you would have sent me away empty handed except the fear of the Almighty, the All Supreme Ruler of my father Isaac had been with me. The Almighty has seen me oppressed and afflicted. He has observed the labor of my hands, and HE has considered. Therefore, last night He decided to reason with you before appointing His Judgment upon you. Laban responded to Jacob saying, your wives are my daughters, these children are my grandchildren, these cattle are my cattle, and all that you see it mine. This day, what can I do onto my daughters and the children they gave birth to? Now, you come. Let us make a covenant. Let you and I make a friendship and an alliance. This covenant will be for a witness between me and you. Jacob spoke to his brethren saying, gather stones. They gathered stones and put them into a pile. Jacob took a stone and set it upon the top, then the pile of stones was established as a memorial. Laban spoke saying, on this day, for a memorial, this pile of stones is a witness between me and Jacob. Laban continued speaking saying, when we are absent one from another, the Almighty will watch over the covenant between me and you. Laban spoke to Jacob, saying, look at this heap of stones. Look at this memorial that I have placed between you and me. No man is between us. If you oppress my daughters or if you take other wives beside my daughters, no man is between us, therefore, only the Almighty is witness between me and you. This heap of stones be witness and this memorial be for a testimony that I will not pass over this memorial to you and you will not pass over this memorial to me for harm. The Almighty, the All Supreme Ruler of Abraham, the Eloheem of Nahor, and the Eloheem of their father, judge between us. By the fear of his father Isaac, Jacob took the oath. Jacob called the name of it Galeed (**Gail-odd**). Laban called it Jegarsahadutha (**Yay-gair**) (**Sah-had-doo-thah**). Then Jacob offered a sacrifice upon the mountain of Gilead, then called his brethren to eat. They did eat bread and stayed all night in the mountain. Laban rose up early in the morning. He kissed his daughters. He kissed his grandsons. He kissed his granddaughter. He praised and adored them. Then, Laban departed away and returned to his own place. Jacob departed from there and went on his way living according to the manner the Almighty appointed to mankind. On his journey back to his father's home, Jacob reached a boundary and he encountered the angels, the prophets, the teachers, and the priests of the Eloheem. They are godly consisting of gods, godlike ones, and goddess that have special works and possessions. They appeared great and mighty. The Eloheem were meeting together in prayer.

When Jacob saw them, he observed them to learn about them. He watched them to see if he could respect them and to see if he could enjoy them. Some of them seemed friendly and some of them seemed hostile. Then, the rulers and judges met Jacob with kindness and entreated him to join them. When they presented themselves to Jacob, while looking at each other in the face, Jacob considered the vision he had been shown. Jacob spoke to his brethren saying, this the host of the Eloheem. Their host is of the stars. They are an army of people travelling like troops. They are an army of people traveling like a flight of locust. In their two camps, they are an army of people with bands of angels, bands of soldiers, and bands of dancers. They have sacred courts, herds of cattle, and tents. Jacob called the name of that place Mahanaim (**Mah-han-nay-yim**). Jacob continued on his way living according to the manner the Almighty appointed to mankind. Jacob sent messengers ahead of him to meet his brother Esau in the land of Seir (**Say-eerh**). Seir is in the country of Edom (**Ay-dome**). Before sending his messengers, Jacob commanded them saying, this is what you will say to lord Esau. Jacob, your fellow servant says I have traveled and lived with Laban, and I have stayed there until now. I have oxen, asses, flocks, men servants, and women servants. In front of me, I have sent messengers to tell you because you are the lord of the land. I hope I can find grace in your sight. The messengers returned to Jacob saying, we came to meet your brother Esau. He is coming to meet you and four hundred men are with him. Jacob became very afraid and distressed. He divided his people and the people that were with him. He divided them, the flocks, the herds, and the camel into two separate bodies.

Jacob spoke to himself saying, if Esau comes to the one company of people, attacks them and kills them, then the other company of people that is left will be able to escape. Jacob spoke to himself saying, to the Almighty, the All Supreme Being, the All Supreme Ruler, who is the All Supreme Ruler of my grandfather Abraham and who is the All Supreme Ruler of my father Isaac, You are the same All Supreme Ruler who spoke to me saying, you return to country, to your brethren, and I will deal well with you. Now, I am insignificant. I am not worthy of the least of Your kindness. I am not worthy of the least of Your faithfulness. I am not worthy of the least of Your goodness and mercy. I am not worthy of all the knowledge, all the stability, all the divine instruction, and all the truth You have shown onto me, your servant, your worshipper. I passed over this descending river, this Jordan (**Yair-dain**) and now I have become two companies of people. I pray and hope You will save me. I pray and hope You will deliver me from sin and guilt. I pray and hope You will deliver me from the trouble of enemies. Because I fear him, I pray and hope You will deliver me from the hand of my brother, from the hand of Esau; unless he comes to attack me and kills me; unless he comes and attacks these mothers with children then kills them. You, O Almighty, spoke to me. You promised me saying, I have accepted you. I will cause you to do what is right. I will be very kind and very good to you. I will cause you to be very happy and successful. In number, I will make the descendants of your posterity, who are of moral quality, like the sand of sea. They will not be numbered because of their multitude. That same night, Jacob rested there and he took that which came to his hand for a gift to his brother Esau. Two hundred she goats, twenty he goats, two hundred female lambs, and twenty rams, thirty nursing camels with their colts, forty cows, ten bulls, twenty she asses, and ten donkeys.

Jacob delivered every group from the herd by themselves into the hand of his servants. Then, Jacob spoke to his servants commanding them saying, go ahead of me and put a space between each of the herds. Jacob commanded the servants at the beginning of the herds saying, when you meet my brother Esau and he asks you, who are you? Where are you going? Who do these herds belong to? Then, you will say, they belong to Jacob, your fellow servant. It is a gift sent to Esau, the lord of the land. Jacob is following behind us. So, Jacob commanded the second set of his servants and the third, and all that followed the herds. He spoke to them saying, when you find Esau, you will speak in this manner to him. You will say, Your fellow servant Jacob is following behind us. Now, Jacob had spoken to himself saying, I will be merciful. I will make an atonement for my sin against him. I will appease him with the gifts that go ahead of me, and afterward I will see the countenance of his face, then maybe he will accept me. Therefore, the gifts went ahead of him. Jacob, himself, stayed and rested that night in the company of his people. Jacob rose up that night and took his wives and his eleven sons, and sent them and everything that he had over the Jabbok (**Yav-boak**) passage. Jacob was left alone, but Jacob was left behind with more than enough. There that night, one human being, a certain man of high degree who was like a champion of mankind wrestled with Jacob. Jacob wrestled this mighty man to the ground. As the dust from the ground flew away into the wind, Jacob grappled with this man. They wrestled and grappled against each other until the rising of the sun. When the man saw he did not have the strength and ability to accomplish victory over Jacob, when the man saw there was no way to overcome Jacob, he got near to Jacob, and laid his hands upon Jacob. To cast Jacob down and defeat him, the man began to violently strike at Jacob's loins, his hips, and the thigh side of the body. Jacob laid his hands upon the man and cast him down and they got back up holding one another. As Jacob continued wrestling him, Jacob's thigh bone came out of its joint, and hurt his nerves, veins, and tendons, but fate befell upon Jacob, at that moment, the man commanded Jacob saying, let me go before the sun rises. Jacob responded saying, I will not let you go unless you bless me with praise and adoration. The man asked Jacob, what is your name? Jacob replied, it is Jacob. The man responded saying, your name, your reputation, your character, your authority, your glory, your honor will no more be Jacob but Israel (**Yis-rhy-ale**) because you are like a powerful king. You have the power to contend with, persevere, and command the Eloheem. You have the power to exert yourself as a king among the Eloheem and as a king among men because you have prevailed over the Eloheem and over men. Jacob spoke to him saying, I hope you will tell me your name. The man responded asking, why is it that you ask me for my name? The man blessed Jacob with praise and adoration. Jacob called the name of the place Penuel (**Pen-oo-ale**) because speaking to himself, he said as this was purposed, I have seen and become acquainted with a godlike one of the Eloheem face to face, my might at battle against his might, my presence at battle against his presence, my countenance at battle against his countenance, my person at battle against his person, my sight at battle against his sight, and my life is preserved. As Jacob passed over Penuel, the sun rose upon him, and he limped upon one side of his thigh. Now, in the company of his household, Jacob lifted up his eyes and looked. Esau was coming toward him with four hundred men under his rule, and they were equipped with weapons. Jacob separated the children. Leah's children were with her.

Rachel's children were with her. The two handmaids' children were them. Jacob put the handmaids' children at the beginning, then Leah and her children after them. He put Rachel and her son Joseph at the end. Jacob bowed himself down to the ground until he came near to his brother, then he was before him. Esau was moving quickly and ran to meet Jacob. Esau embraced Jacob into his arms with his hands. He touched Jacob gently and kissed him, then they wept. When Esau lifted up his eyes, he saw the women and children. He observed them and considered. As they were looking at each other's' face, he wanted to find out if he could respect them and enjoy them. Esau spoke to Jacob asking, who are these persons with you? Jacob answered saying, the children that the Almighty has given your fellow servant by HIS favor and mercy. Then the handmaidens with their children came near to them and bowed themselves. Then, Leah with her children came near to them and bowed themselves. Then Rachel and her son Joseph came to them and bowed themselves. Esau spoke to Jacob asking, as I was coming to meet you, what did you mean by sending me all these flocks and herds? Jacob answered saying, they were a gift to find favor and acceptance in the sight of the lord of this land. Esau spoke to Jacob saying, my brother, I have enough. Keep what you have for yourself. Jacob responded by saying, no. Now, if I have found favor and acceptance in your sight, then by my hand, I pray that you receive my present. To see joy on your face, to see you pleased with me, would be as though I had seen joy on the face of the Almighty and He was pleased with me. I pray that you take the blessing I have brought to you. I hope that you take the praise and adoration I have brought you because the Almighty has been merciful to me and has dealt with me according to His kindness. Also, I have enough. Jacob continued to urge Esau, then Esau took possession of Jacob's gifts. Esau spoke to Jacob saying, let us take our journey, let us go together and I will go ahead of you. Jacob responded to Esau saying, the lord of the land has experience. You understand that the children are delicate and faint-hearted. You understand that the flocks and herds with their young are with me. You understand that if men overdrive the herds and flocks for one day, they will all die. I hope that the lord of the land will go on ahead of his fellow servant. I will gently lead myself along the journey according to the pace of the cattle that is ahead of me, then the children will be able to endure until I come onto the lord of the land in Seir (**Say-eer**). Esau spoke to Jacob saying, now, let me leave you with some of these men that are with me. Jacob responded asking, why do I need them? Let me find favor and acceptance in the sight of the lord of the land. On that day, Esau went back on his way to Seir. Jacob journeyed to Succoth (**Soo-koath**). There, Jacob built a house for himself and his family. He built booths for his cattle. He built a temple with a court. Jacob named this place, he called it to be the same name, Succoth. From there Jacob came to Shalem (**Shah-lame**). Shalem is in the land of Canaan. It is a city of excitement, of terror, and of anguish. It is also called the city of Shechem. Shechem was son of Hamor. Hamor is king of the Hivites (**Hev-vee**). Jacob pitched his tent outside the city. There, Jacob bought a flat piece of land with a field for one hundred pieces of money from the descendants of Hamor. On this piece of land, Jacob appointed officers and deputies. He appointed them to be stationed there. He set up and established an altar there. Jacob called the altar (**Shah-dye**) meaning the Almighty.

Then Jacob chose and invited guests to preach to them. Jacob preached the authority, the reputation, the honor, the glory, and the character of the Almighty, the All Supreme Being, the All Supreme Ruler, the Creator of all things. Dinah (**Dee-nah**), the daughter of Jacob's wife Leah (**Lay-ah**) considered the daughters of the land and went out to learn about them. Dinah wanted to see if she could respect them and enjoy learning about them, therefore, she went out to present herself to them. Shechem (**Shak- em**) is the son of Hamor (**Ham-more**). He was the prince of the country. When he saw Dinah present herself to the daughters of the land, he considered. He observed her and gave his attention to her. He wanted to see if he could respect her and enjoy learning about her, therefore, he appeared and presented himself to her. Shechem mishandled Dinah's humbleness and gentleness. He spoke humbly to her, but he humiliated and hurt her. He defiled her. Shechem took possession of her and ravished her. He made her lie down to have sexual relations with him, then he fell in love with Dinah. He spoke to her with care, and his words were kind. He stayed with Dinah and followed her closely. Shechem spoke to his father Hamor saying, you will get me this young woman for me to be my wife. Now, Jacob stopped what he was doing to listen to a report from a witness. Jacob listened with interest as the witness spoke aloud. Then, Jacob understood. He heard that Shechem had defiled his daughter Dinah. Jacob's sons were with his cattle in the field. Jacob held his peace until they came back from the field with his cattle. Hamor, the father of Shechem arranged to meet Jacob and went out to speak with him. When the sons of Jacob heard the report from the witness, they came out of the field. They were hurt and displeased. They were worried about Shechem's form of worship. They were angry and grieved in pain. They began to become very angry because Shechem had brought senselessness, disgrace, immorality, and wickedness onto the house of Jacob by forcibly lying in sexual relations with Jacob's daughter. This is a thing that needs not to be done nor accomplished. Hamor arranged to meet with them and he spoke to Jacob saying, the heart of my son Shechem delights in loving your daughter. His heart is attached to her. His desire and love is set upon her. I pray that you will give her to him to be his wife. You will make your marriages with us. You will give your daughters onto us and take our daughters onto you. You will live with us and the land will be in front of you. Live and trade in the land. Take your possessions from in this land. Shechem spoke to Jacob and Dinah's brothers saying, let me find favor and acceptance in your eyes. Whatever you will ask of me, I will give it. Ask me. There is no such thing as too many gifts and presents because I will give you according to what you ask of me. Only, give Dinah to me to be my wife. The sons of Jacob answered Shechem and his father Hamor deceitfully because Shechem had mishandled and defiled their sister Dinah. They spoke them saying, we cannot do this thing. We cannot give our sister to a man that is uncircumcised, who has not circumcised his flesh by cutting off his foreskin. This would be shame and disgrace onto us. If you become as we are, and every male of you circumcise his flesh by cutting off his foreskin, in this, we will agree with your request. Then we will give our daughters to you and we will take your daughters to us. We will live with you and we will become one and the same people of a nation. But, if you do not obey what we request from you, to be circumcised in the flesh by cutting off your foreskin, then we will take our sister and we will be gone away.

Their words were pleasing to Hamor and his son Shechem. Shechem did not hold off from nor put away doing this thing because he delighted in Jacob's daughter; and Shechem was glorified with more honor than all the house of his father. King Hamor and Shechem came into the court of their city and conversed with the men of their city. They spoke to their men saying, the men of the house of Jacob are at peace with us. Let them live in the land and trade in it because the land is large enough for them. Let us marry their daughters and let us give our daughters to them for marriage. They will live with us to be one and the same people, but only on one condition, if every male among us be circumcised in the flesh as they are circumcised. Will not their cattle and their substance and every beast of them be ours? Let us agree to their request and they will live with us. All of them that were in the court of the city listened to king Hamor and to Shechem. Then, every male that left out of the city gate was circumcised. On the third day, when the men of Hamor were sore from circumcision, it came to pass, two of Dinah's brothers, two of Jacob's sons, Simeon and Levi took possession of their sword. Then, in confidence, they carelessly and boldly came upon the city. They attacked and killed all the males. They killed king Hamor and prince Shechem with the edge of their sword. They took Dinah out of Shechem's house and departed away. Because prince Shechem had defiled their sister, the sons of Jacob came and plundered the whole city. They took possession of their sheep, their oxen, their donkeys, all that was in the city, and all that was in their fields. They took all their wealth. They took all their little ones, and their wives captive. They plundered all that was in the house of Hamor. Jacob spoke to his sons Simeon (**Shem-own**) and Levi (**Lay-vee**), saying, you have cause a disturbance. You have caused a calamity. You have stirred up trouble against me, and you have cause me to stink of wickedness among the Canaanites (**Kennah-a-nee**), among the Perizzites (**Pear-rah-zee**), and among the inhabitants of the land. Now, because I am fewer in number, they will assemble and gather themselves against me to kill me. Me and my house will be destroyed. They responded to Jacob asking, should we have let him deal with our sister like a prostitute? The Almighty visited and spoke to Jacob saying, I am the ALMIGHTY, the ALL SUPREME BEING, the ALL SUPREME RULER, the CREATOR of all things, I appeared to you when you fled from the face of your brother Esau. Now, arise and go outside the city of Luz to Bahyith Shahdye (**Bah-yith Shah-dye**). You will live there. There, you will build and set up an altar to honor ME. Jacob spoke to his household and all that were with him, warning them, commanding them saying, reject the Eloheem. Rebel and reject their gods, their goddesses, their angels, their rulers, their judges, and their mighty ones. Depart from their ways and eliminate their way of living from among you. They are foreign gods of vanity, therefore, reject and rebel against any god among you. All gods are of the stranger. All gods are of the heathen. Depart from all their ways and remove them from among you. Do not contaminate yourselves with them. Be morally clean and ceremonially innocent. Present yourselves as pure. For the better, change your garments and clothing. Now, let us arise and, we will go to **Bahyith Shahdye**. I will build and set up an altar there to honor the Almighty, the All Supreme Being, the All Supreme Ruler, the Creator of all things. It is He, the Almighty, who answered me in the time of my distress. It was He, the Almighty, who was with me wherever I went on my journey.

They gave Jacob all the gods and idols of the Eloheem that were in their hands under their care. They gave Jacob all their foreign gods of vanity that are of the stranger and heathen. They gave Jacob all the jewelry and earrings that were in their ears. Jacob hid them secretly under an oak tree that was by the city of Shechem (**Shahk-em**). Then, they journeyed together. The fear, the terror, and dread of the Almighty were upon the cities that were all around them. The people of the cities did not pursue after the sons of Jacob nor chase after any of those that were with them. In the land of Canaan, Jacob and all the people that were with him came to Luz (**Looz**). They settled outside the city in Bahyith Shah-dye. Jacob built and set up an altar there. He chose and invited guests to be preached to. Then, Jacob preached the honor, the reputation, the character, the authority, and the glory of the Almighty. Now, as a penalty of neglecting wise conduct and good morals, Rebekah's nurse Deborah died prematurely. She was put to death. She was killed by a warlock magician of necromancy. She was buried under an oak tree in **Bayith Shahdye**. The name of the tree was called Allonbachuth (**Al-loan-bah-hooth**), the oak of weeping. When Jacob came out of Padan journeying to Shalem (**Shah-lame**), in a dream, the Almighty appeared visible before Jacob again. The Almighty blessed him. The Almighty spoke to Jacob saying, I am the Almighty, the All Supreme Being, the All Supreme Ruler, the Creator of all things. I will cause you to be fruitful and multiply to become numerous in number in the land. A nation of people, of My purpose, of My service, as an organized body of people, your people will become a nation, and they will invade the land with war against evil counsel, but they will assemble themselves in evil counsel. A nation of returning exiles, of a multitude of nations, of My purpose, of My service, as an organized body of people will invade the land with a war against evil counsel, and they will assemble in My counsel. Both these nations of people and their royal kings will come from your loins. The land that I gave to your grandfather Abraham is the same land I gave to your father Isaac, and this will be the same land I will give to you. It will be the same land I give to your children, to your children's offspring, to your children's offspring's descendants, to your descendants' posterity. And of your posterity's descendants, to a people of moral quality and a practitioner of MY righteousness. Then, the Almighty departed and ascended from the place where HE talked to Jacob. In the same place where the Almighty spoke to Jacob, Jacob built and set up another memorial of stone and poured a drink offering upon it, then he poured oil upon it. Jacob chose and invited guests to preach to them. Then Jacob preached and proclaimed the authority, the honor, the character, the reputation, and the glory of the Almighty, the All Supreme Being, the All Supreme Ruler. Jacob called this place (**Shah-dye-Bah-yith-Shah-dye**), the Almighty of the house of the Almighty because by vision, the Almighty, the All Supreme Being, the All Supreme Ruler appeared and presented HIMSELF face to face with Jacob again. Therefore, the name of the place where the Almighty spoke to him again is called **Shah-dye Bahyith Shah-dye**. Then, as he and those with him journeyed from Shah-dye Bahyith Shah-dye, when there was a little way to go to reach Ephrath (**Eph-roth**), Rachel began to have labor pains. While Rachel was in hard pain from the difficult labor, it came to pass, her midwife spoke to her saying, do not fear, you will have this son also.

As her soul was leaving her body, as she was dying, Rachel called the boy's name Benoni (**Bane**), but his father Jacob called him Benjamin (**Ben-yah-meen**). Rachel died and was buried on the journey to Ephrath which is before Bethlehem (**Bayth-lac-em**). Jacob built and set up a memorial of stone upon her grave and it is the same memorial stone of Rachel's grave to this day. Jacob continued to journey and spread his tent beyond the castles and tower of Edar (**Ay-dare**). The tower of Edar is near Bethlehem. Now, the sons of Jacob were twelve in number. When Jacob lived in the land, it came to pass, his firstborn Reuben went and lay down in sexual relations with his father's concubine Bilhah (**Bil-hah**). Jacob stopped what he was doing and listened with interest to the report from a witness. Now, the sons of Leah (**Lay-ah**) were Reuben (**Reh-oo-vain**), Simeon (**Shem-own**), Levi (**Leh-vee**), Judah (**Yeh-who-dah**), Issachar (**Yis-hah-har**), and Zebulun (**Zev-voo-loon**). The sons of Rachel were Joseph (**Yo-safe**) and Benjamin (**Ben-yah-meen**). The sons of Rachel's handmaid Bilhah were Dan (**Don**) and Naphtali (**Naph-tah-lee**). The sons of Leah's handmaid Zilpah were Gad (**God**) and Asher (**Ah-share**). Zilpah's sons were born to Jacob in Padan. Jacob came to his father Isaac in Mamre (**Mam-ray**) at the city of Kirjah Arbah (**Keer-yah**) (**Ar-bah**). Kirjah Arbah is the name of the city before it was called Hebron. This is where Abraham and Isaac traveled and lived. Being old and full of days, Isaac lived to be one hundred eighty years old. Then, as his spirit departed, Isaac took his last breath and died. All his people were assembled and gathered to him. His sons, Esau and Jacob buried him. These are the generations of Esau (**Ay-sav**). Esau is also known as is Edom (**Ay-dome**). Esau took possession of women to be for wives. He took some from the daughters of Canaan (Ken-ah-an). There was Adah (Ah-dah). She is the daughter of Elon (**Ay-loan**), the Hittite (Haith). There was Aholibamah (**Ah-holy-vah-mah**). She is the daughter of Anah (**Ah-nah**). Anah is the daughter of Zibeon (**Sev-oan**), the Hivite (**Hev-vee**). There was Ishmael's daughter Bashemath (**Bos-math**). She is the sister of Nebajoth. Bashemath is Ishmael's (**Yish-ma-el**) daughter, and sister of Nebajoth (**Nev-vee-ah**). Nebajoth is a son of Ishmael. Adah (**Ay-dah**) gave birth to Eliphaz (**El-lee-phaz**) for Esau (**Ay-sav**). Bashemath gave birth to Reuel (**Ray-oo-ale**) for Esau. Aholibamah gave birth to Jeush (**Yay-oosh**), then Jaalam (**Yah-lam**), then, Korah (**Kor-rakh**). These are the sons of Esau that were born to him in the land of Canaan. Esau's wealth and Jacob's riches were too much to allow them to dwell together, and the land where they lived in as strangers could not support them because of all their livestock and cattle. Esau took his wives, his sons, his daughters, all the persons of his house, all his cattle, all his Behemah (**Ba-hay-mah**), and, all his substance he got in the land of Canaan, then he went into the country away from the face of his brother Jacob. Esau went to live in the mountain of Seir (**Say-eer**). These are the generations of Esau. Esau is the chief ancestor and progenitor of the Edomites in the mountain of Seir. These are the names of Esau's sons. Eliphaz (**El-lee-phaz**) is the son of Esau and Adah. Reuel (**Ray-oo-ale**) is the son of Esau and Bashemath. The sons of Eliphaz were Teman (**Tay-mon**), then Omar (**O-marh**), then Zepho (**Seph-pho**), then, Gatam (**Gat-tom**), then Kenaz (**Ken-naz**). Timna was the concubine of Eliphaz and she gave birth to Amalek (**Am-mah-lake**). These were the grandsons of Esau's wife Adah. These are the sons of Reuel. Firstborn is Nahath (**Nah-hath**), then Zerah (**Zeh-rahk**), then Shammah (**Shah-mah**), then Mizzah (**Miz-zay**). These were the grandsons of Esau's wife Bashemath (**Bos-math**).

These were the governors out of the sons of Esau. From Eliphaz, the firstborn son of Esau, there was governor Teman, governor Omar (**O-marh**), governor Zepho (**Sef-pho**), governor Kenaz (**Ken-naz**), governor Korah (**Kor-rahk**), governor Gatam (**Gat-tom**), and governor Amalek (Am-mah-lek). These are the governors that came from Eliphaz in the land of Edom. These are the dukes that came of Eliphaz in the land of Edom. These were the sons and grandsons of Esau's wife Adah. These are the sons of Esau's son Reuel. Governor Nahath, governor Zerah, governor Shammah, and governor Mizzah. These are the dukes that came from Reuel in the land of Edom. These are the sons of Esau's wife Bashemath. These are the sons of Esau's wife Aholibamah. Governor Jeush, governor Jaalam, and governor Korah. These were the dukes that came from Esau's wife Aholibamah. These are the dukes and the governors of Edom. These are the sons of Seir, (**Say-eer**) the Horite (**Hor-ree**), who inhabited the land before Esau and his descendants. There is Lotan (**Low-tawn**), an Idumean. There is Shobal (**Show-val**). Shobal is one of the dukes of the Horites. There is Zibeon (**Sev-voan**), a son of Seir, whose granddaughter is Aholibamah, and she married Esau. There is Anah (**An-nah**), a Horite chief. Anah is the son of Zibeon. Anah is the father of Aholibamah. There is Dishon (**Dee-shown**). Dishon is the son of Anah. There is Ezer (**Ay-zair**), an aboriginal Idumean. Ezer is a chief of the Horites. There is Dishan (**Dee-shawn**). These are the dukes of the Horites. These are the children of Seir in the land of Edom. The children of Lotan were Hori (**Hore-ree**), then Hemam (**Hey-mom**). Lotan's sister was Timna (**Tim-nah**). The children of Shobal (Show-vol). Shobal is the second son of Seir. Shobal's firstborn is Alvan (**Al-von**). Alvan was a tall aboriginal Idumean. Shobal's second son is Manahath (**Mon-nah-hath**), then Ebal (**Ay-vol**), then Shepho (**Shef-fo**), then Onam (**O-nom**). These are the children of Zibeon (**Sev-voan**). Zibeon is the father of Ajah (**Ah-yah**) and Anah (**An-nah**). This was that Anah that found the hot springs in the wilderness as he fed the donkeys of his father Zibeon. These are the children of Dishon. There is Hemdan (**Hem-don**), an Idumean. There is Eshban (**Esh-bon**), an aboriginal Idumean. There is Ithran (**Yith-run**). There is Cheran (**Kay-run**), an aboriginal Idumean. The children of Ezer (**A-zair**) are Bilhan (Bil-hun), then Zaavan (**Za-ah-von**), an aboriginal Idumean, then Akan (**Ak-con**), an aboriginal Idumean. The children of Dishan (**Dee-shawn**) are Uz (**ootz**). Uz had regions of land named after him. There is Aran (**Air-run**). The dukes that came from the Horites are Lotan, Shobal, Zibeon, Anah, Dishon, Ezer, and Dishan. Before any king reigned over the house of Jacob, these are kings that reigned in the land of Edom. Bela (**Bel-lah**), the son of Beor (**Bay-ore**) reigned in Edom. He had a capital city of excitement, of terror, and of anguish. It was a place where robbers lurked. The name of his city was called Dinhabah (**Den-hah-vah**). Jobab (**Yo-vov**) was a king of Edom. As a penalty of neglecting wise conduct and good morals, he died prematurely. He was put to death by a warlock magician of necromancy. Husham (**Who-shum**) an Idumean, from the land of Temani (**Tay-mun**), reigned in his place. As a penalty of neglecting wise conduct and good morals, Husham died prematurely. He was put to death by a warlock magician of necromancy. Hadad, (**Hah-dad**) was the son of Bedad (**Bah-dad**). Hadad killed Midian in the field of Moab. Midian (**Mid-ee-on**) was a son of Abraham. Hadad reigned in the place of Husham. He had a city of excitement, of terror, and of anguish.

The name of city was called Avith (**Av-veeth**), and it also called the city of Hadad Ben-Bedad. As a penalty of neglecting wise conduct and good morals, he died prematurely. Hadad was put to death by a warlock magician of necromancy. Samlah (**Sam-lah**) of Masrekah (**Mass-reh-kah**) reigned in his place. As a penalty of neglecting wise conduct and good morals, Samlah died prematurely. He was put to death by a warlock magician of necromancy. By the river, Saul (**Shah-ool**) of Rehoboth (**Rekh-ho-voth**) reigned in his place. As a penalty of neglecting wise conduct and good morals, Samlah died prematurely. He was put to death by a warlock magician of necromancy. When Saul died, Baalhanan, (**Bay-al-hah-nun**), reigned in his place. Baalhanan. His name meant Baal is gracious. It was believed he possessed the grace of Baal. Baalhanan was the son of Achbor (**Akh-bore**). As a penalty of neglecting wise conduct and good morals, Baalhanan died prematurely. He was put to death by a warlock magician of necromancy. Hadar (**Hah-dad**) reigned in his place. Hadar had a city of excitement, of terror, and of anguish. The name of his capital city was Pau (**Pah-oo**). His wife's name was Mehetabel (**Mah-hay-tav-ale**). Mehetabel was the granddaughter of Matred (Mat-raid). Matred was the daughter of Mezahab (My). These are the names of the dukes that came from Esau, according to their families in their places. There was duke Timnah (**Tim-nah**), duke Alvah (**Al-vah**), duke Jetheth (**Yeth-thayth**), duke Aholibamah (**Ah-ho-lee-vah-mah**), duke Elah (**Ay-lah**), duke Pinon (**Pee-known**), duke Kenaz (**Ka-naz**), duke Teman (**Tay-mon**), duke Mibzar (**Miv-zar**), duke Magdiel (**Mag-dee-ale**), and Iram (**Ee-rum**). These were the dukes of Edom according to their habitations in the land of their possession. The chief ancestor and the progenitor of the Edomites is Esau. Jacob lived in the land the land of Canaan where his father and his forefather was a stranger. Jacob's son Joseph was seventeen years old. Jacob loved Joseph more than all his children because Joseph was the first son of his very old age. Jacob made Joseph a coat of many different colors. When Joseph's brothers saw that their father loved Joseph more than all his brothers, they became completely hateful of him. They hated him as an enemy, therefore, they could not think good about him nor speak peace, prosperity, and good health toward him. Afterwards, after Joseph finished feeding his father's flock with his brothers. Joseph came to his father Jacob. He told Jacob his brothers were being evil. He told Jacob that his brothers were causing him to be distressed, unhappy, and miserable by whispering false statements and defaming him. As Joseph was sleeping, he dreamed and had a vision in his dream. He told it to his brothers and they hated him even more. Joseph spoke to them saying, I pray that you hear about my dream. Now, we were tying and binding sheaves of grain in the field. My sheaf arose and stood upright. Then all your sheaves stood round about mine and bowed down to my sheaf. Mocking, Joseph's brothers asked him, will you rule over us? Will you have power and authority over us? Now, his brothers hated him even more because of his dream, and the words that he spoke. Then Joseph dreamed and had another vision. He told it to his brothers. He told them saying, I had another dream, the sun, the moon, and eleven stars bowed down to me in homage. It was like angels worshipping god. Then Joseph told it to his father Jacob. Jacob asked Joseph, what is this dream? Will I, your mother, and your brethren bow down ourselves to the earth to worship you?

Jacob scolded him as from a father to a son, then Jacob corrected what Joseph was corrupting. Jacob kept Joseph's words within the limits of the Covenant and within the Commandments of the Almighty. Joseph's brothers became very jealous. They became very angry and envious of him, but Jacob was a watchman, therefore, he started waiting and watching for what Joseph had spoken of. Afterwards, Joseph's brothers went to feed their father's flock in Shechem. Jacob asked Joseph, why are you not feeding the flock with your brothers in Shechem? Come here and I will send you to them. Joseph answered Jacob saying, I am here. Jacob responded by saying, I pray that you go to them and see whether it is going well with your brothers. See if it is going well with the flocks. Bring your report back here to me. Then, Jacob sent Joseph out of the valley of Hebron and Joseph journeyed to Shechem. A certain man found him and saw that he was wandering in a field. The man asked Joseph, what is your desire? What are you searching for? Joseph answered, I desire to find my brothers. I desire to see them face to face. Please, tell me where they feed their flocks. The man spoke to Joseph saying, I listened to them. I paid attention to them and heard them speak to one another. Now, they have departed away from here. They said, let us go to Dothan (**Dough-thah-yen**), the place of two water wells. Then, Joseph pursued his brothers, and found them in Dothan. When they saw him far off, they conspired to deceive him, even right before he came near to them, they conspired against him. They conspired to kill him. They spoke to one another saying, look, the prophetic dreamer is coming. Look, the dreamer who dreams that he will be a king, a master and a lord of all inhabitants is coming. Come now.

Let us kill him then throw him into some grave. We will say that some evil beast has devoured him. We will see what becomes of his prophetic dreams and visions. Joseph's oldest brother Reuben was listening to them. He was paying attention to them. Reuben saved his brothers from sin and guilt. He delivered Joseph out of their hands by saying, let us not kill him. Reuben spoke to his brothers saying, we do not need to kill him. We do not need to shed any of his blood. I saw a pit in the wilderness and we can throw him in that hole, but we will not place our hands on him to shed his blood. We will get him out of our hands, and we will not bring him back to his father again. When Joseph had come near his brothers. As he was looking at them in their faces, they stripped Joseph and took his coat of many colors that he was wearing. His brothers took him and threw him into an empty pit in the wilderness. Now, the pit was empty and there was no water in it, but it was near a way. Then they sat down to eat some food. When they lifted their eyes to see, they saw a company of travelling Ishmaelites with camels coming from Gilead (**Gil-odd**). They were carrying spices, balm, and myrrh. They were traveling toward Egypt. Judah (**Yeh-who-dah**) spoke to his brothers saying, Joseph is our brother, what profit is it if we kill our brother in secret? Joseph is our flesh and blood, what do we gain by hiding his murder? What do we profit by hiding his murderers? Judah continued speaking saying, come, let us sell him to the Ishmaelites. Joseph's brothers came to an agreeance, and they were content with their decision. As they conspired against Joseph, Midianite merchantmen passed by the pit where Joseph was in. They lifted Joseph from out of the hole and sold Joseph to the travelling Ishmaelites for twenty pieces of silver. The Ishmaelites brought Joseph into the land of the Egyptians.

When Reuben returned to the pit, he looked and saw that his brother Joseph was not in the pit, then from sorrow, Reuben began to rip and tear his clothes. Reuben returned to his brothers and spoke to them saying, the boy is not there. I do not know where he has gone. I do not know where he has been taken. Then, Joseph's brothers took his coat of many colors, and they departed away. They dipped the coat in the blood of a kid goat they had killed. Then, they brought the coat to their father Jacob. They spoke to Jacob saying, we found this coat of many colors. Do you know if this is your son's coat or not? Jacob recognized it. He spoke to his sons saying, this is my son's coat and an evil beast has devoured him. Without a doubt, Joseph has been torn into pieces by an evil beast. In grief and sorrow, Jacob began to tear his clothes. Jacob put sackcloth on around the sides of his body, then for many days, he mourned for his son Joseph. All Jacobs sons and all his daughters rose to comfort him, but he refused to be comforted. He declared to them saying, I will go down into my grave mourning my son. This is how Joseph's father wept for him. The Midianites (**Mid-ee-ah-neen**), sold Joseph to the Ishmaelites then, once in Egypt, the Ishmaelites sold him to Potiphar(**Po-tee-fair**). Potiphar was an officer of the Egyptian Pharaoh, and a captain of the Pharaoh's army. He was a chief executioner of Pharaoh. At that time, Judah (**Yeh-who-dah**) had departed away from his brethren and went to a lower region in the land to spread himself out. On his journey, in the afternoon, he turned in to meet a great man of high degree. This man was a champion to the people and a servant of mankind. This man was a certain Adullamite (**Ad-du-lah-mee**) inhabiting Adullam

(**Ad-du-lum**). He had a reputation of glory, honor, and authority. His name was Hirah (**Hay-rah**), and he was Judah's friend. There, Judah was caused to see a young woman. When she appeared, Judah gazed at her. He watched her and considered. Judah advised himself he wanted to have experiences with her and learn about her. As Judah presented himself, they looked at each other in face. She was the daughter of a great Canaanite man of high degree. This man was a champion to the people and a servant of mankind. This man had a reputation of glory, honor, and authority. His name was Shuah (**Sho-akh**). Judah went in to Shuah's daughter with sexual affections and took this woman for a wife. She became pregnant and gave birth to a son. Judah chose and invited guests. He preached about the Almighty. He brought his son before them and called the name of his child Er (**Air**). Judah's wife became pregnant again and she gave birth to another son. She chose and invited guests. She brought her child before them and called his name Onan (**O-non**). Judah's wife became pregnant again and she gave birth to another son. They chose and invited guests. They brought their child before them and called his name Shelah (**Sheh-lah**). In the land Canaan, Shelah was born at a place called Chezib (**Keh-zeev**). Er found a woman to be a wife. Her name was Tamar (**Tah-mar**). Judah's firstborn Er was very evil in the sight of the Almighty. Er was causing great pain, great unhappiness, and great misery. Therefore, the Almighty, the All Supreme Being, the All Supreme Ruler had him killed. As a penalty for neglecting wise conduct and good morals, Er died prematurely. He was put to death by a warlock magician of necromancy. Judah spoke to his son Onan, and commanded him saying, you go in to your brother Er's wife with sexual affections and marry her. You will have children with her to your brother. You will raise them up to be strong and successful. You will establish them to accomplish good.

nan knew that these children will not be his. He did go in with sexual affections to Tamar, but Onan spilled his semen on the ground, unless he should give children to his brother. This thing that Onan did was evil in the sight of the Almighty. He displeased the Almighty, and it grieved the Almighty's SPIRIT. Therefore, the Almighty had Onan killed. As a penalty for neglecting wise conduct and good morals, Onan died prematurely. He was put to death by a warlock magician of necromancy. Judah spoke to his daughter in law Tamar, and commanded her saying, remain a widow at your father's house until my son Shelah is grown up, unless he dies also as his brothers have. Tamar went away and lived in her father's house. Over the process of time, Judah's wife, the daughter of Shuah died. As a penalty for neglecting wise conduct and good morals, she died prematurely. She was put to death by a warlock magician of necromancy. Judah was stirred up. Suffering from grief, he destroyed the enemy. He cut off their flocks of sheep and their multitude of cattle. Judah sighed within himself and was moved to pity. He regretted comforting himself by revenge. Judah repented, then he found comfort and compassion within himself. He and his friend Hirah, the Adullamite went a place called Timnath (**Tim-nah**). Someone spoke to Tamar saying, your father in law in going to Timnah to shear his sheep. She understood that Judah's son Shelah was grown up, but she had not been given to him for a wife. She took off her widow's garments and covered her face with a veil. She covered herself in disguise and sat in an open area by the road to Timnath. Judah saw her and considered. He gazed at her and observed her. On the road he was journeying on, he turned in to her. He presented himself to her and looked at her face. Because her face was covered, Judah thought she was a harlot. He valued her as a prostitute. Judah did not know that she was his daughter in law. He spoke to her saying, I hope you will let me go with you to come in to you with sexual affections. She responded asking, what will you give me so you can come in to me with sexual affections? Judah answered saying, I will send you a kid goat from my flock. She asked, until you send it, will you give me a pledge? Judah responded asking, what pledge can I give you? She answered, saying, you can give me your signet ring, your bracelets, and the staff that is in your hand. Judah gave it to her, then he came in to her with sexual affections. She became pregnant by him. She arose and departed away. She removed her veil from off her face and put on the garments of her widowhood. Judah sent the kid by the hand of his friend Hirah, the Adullamite, and to receive his pledge back from the woman's hand, but Hirah did not find her. Then, he asked the men of that place saying, where is the harlot that was sitting in the open area by the road? They answered saying, there was no harlot in this place. He returned to Judah and spoke to him saying, I cannot find her. The men of the place spoke to me saying, there was no harlot in this place. Judah responded to Hirah saying, unless we be shamed, let this woman take it to her because I have sent this goat and you have not found her. After about three months, it was told to Judah that his daughter in law Tamar played the harlot, and now she is with a child by whoredom. Judah spoke and commanded saying, bring her forth and let her be set on fire and completely burnt up. Before she was brought forth to be set on fire, she sent the signet ring, the bracelets, and the staff along with word to her father in law Judah saying, I pray that you discern what man this signet ring, these bracelets, and this staff belongs to. I am with child by the man whose these things belong to.

Judah acknowledged them and spoke saying, she has been more righteous than me. I did not give her to my son Shelah as a promised. She was set free. Now, Judah did not go in to her with sexual affections again. At the time of her pregnancy, Tamar looked and saw twins were in her womb. At the time of her labor, as she was giving birth to a child, the first one put out his finger, and the midwife took a scarlet thread and tied it upon his finger to remind her that one came out first, but his finger returned back into the womb and his brother came out instead. The midwife spoke to herself asking, how have you come forth out of the womb? This bursting forth is upon you. Judah and Tamar chose and invited guests. He preached about the Almighty. He brought his child before them and called his name Pharez. (**Pair-retz**). Now, Potiphar owned Joseph, but the Almighty was with Joseph (**Yo-seph**). While Joseph was in the house of Potiphar(**Po-tee-fair**), the Egyptian, Joseph served him and the Almighty caused Joseph to progress into a successful and prosperous man. Potiphar paid attention to Joseph and observed him. Joseph had a beautiful appearance and his body had a beautiful form. Joseph was well favored. In the sight of others, he saw Joseph was enjoyed and respected. Potiphar considered that the Almighty was with Joseph. Potiphar considered that the All Supreme Being, the Almighty caused everything in Joseph's hand and everything that was under his authority to prosper. On all sides, Joseph served Potiphar, and Joseph found favor and acceptance in Potiphar's sight. Potiphar made Joseph the steward of his household affairs, his prison, his animals, and everything that Potiphar put into his hand. From the time Potiphar made Joseph overseer in his house and over all that he had, it came to pass, for Joseph's sake, the Almighty blessed Potiphar's house to be praised and adored. The Almighty's blessing of praise and adoration was upon all Potiphar had in his house and in the fields he owned. Except the food he ate, Potiphar left all that he had under Joseph's authority, and Potiphar did not understand why he had done this. After these things, it came to pass, Potiphar's wife cast her eyes upon Joseph. She commanded Joseph saying, you will lie with me in sexual relations. Joseph refused her. Joseph spoke to her saying, look, my lord does not know nor does he understand, neither does he consider what is under my authority in his house, but he has given all that he has into my hand under my authority. In this house, your husband has not withheld anything from me but you. Under your husband, in this house, there is no one greater than I. You are his wife, how can I do a great evil as the Eloheem and sin against the Almighty. It came to pass, as she spoke to Joseph day by day, he did not listen to her, he did not give his attention to her, he did not obey her request for him to lie with her in sexual relations, nor did he honor her demand for him to be with her. About this time, it came to pass, Joseph went into the house to perform his job and there were no men within the house. She grabbed Joseph by his garment commanding him saying, you will lie with me in sexual relations, but Joseph ran out of the house and escaped her grasp. He left his garment in her hand. When she saw that Joseph left his garment in her hand, when Joseph had gone out of the house, she called to the men of her house. She spoke to them saying, look Potiphar(**Po-tee-fair**), you have brought a great man, an Eberite (**Ay-vair-ee**), into our home to mock us. He came in onto me to lie with me in sexual relations, and I cried out with a loud voice. When he listened to me lift my voice up, when he heard me cry out aloud, he ran away out of the house and he left his garment with me.

She kept Joseph's garment with her until her husband, Joseph's owner, Potiphar came home. Then, she spoke to her husband saying, your servant, that Eberite you brought into our home came in onto me to lie down with me in sexual relations. As I lifted up my voice, as he heard me cry out aloud, he ran out of the house and left his garment with me. When Potiphar heard these words from his wife, he became angry and furious. Potiphar found Joseph and took possession of him, then cast him into his dungeon where the king's prisoners were restrained. Now, Joseph was there in a dungeon, but the Almighty was with Joseph. The Almighty showed him mercy. The Almighty caused Joseph to gain acceptance and favor in the sight of the dungeon's watchman, the captain who was in charge of watching over the prisoners. The watchman of the dungeon appointed all the prisoners that were in the prison to be under Joseph's authority. Whatever the prisoners did there was by Joseph's approval. The watchman of the dungeon did not watch over anything that was under Joseph's authority because the Almighty was with Joseph and anything that Joseph did, the Almighty caused it to succeed and prosper. After these things, it came to pass, the chief butler who gave water and potions for the royal king of Egypt to drink, and the chief baker who cooked and baked food for the royal king of Egypt sinned against their lord, the royal king of Egypt. They had wandered away from living according to the royal king of Egypt. The Pharaoh, the royal king of Egypt was very displeased with both these officers of his great house. The Pharaoh put himself into a rage and his anger was bursting out against them. Therefore, they were punished for their unclean acts against the royal king of Egypt. He appointed them to be put in the dungeon. He put them in the dungeon under the authority of the captain of the prison guard in the same place where Joseph was restrained to. The captain of the prison guard appointed them to be under the charge of Joseph because Joseph served the captain of the prison guard. They remained there in the dungeon under Joseph's charge for a season of that year. In the dungeon, on the same night, both the chief baker and the chief butler dreamed. Both of them had a dream with prophetic meaning. According to both their dreams, these dreams needed to be interpreted. In the morning, Joseph advised himself to go to them to learn about them. In the sight of others, Joseph presented himself to them. He came near to them and looked at their faces. Both of them were not happy. In the dungeon of Pharaoh's house, Joseph asked both these officers of the Pharaoh saying, why are you two so sad today? Both of them responded to Joseph saying, we dreamed a prophetic dream, and there is no interpreter of it. Joseph responded to them asking, does not interpretations belong to the Eloheem? Then, Joseph declared saying, interpretations do not belong to the Eloheem. I pray that both of you tell your dreams to me. Tell me everything exactly as you saw it. The chief butler told his dream to Joseph saying, a vine was before me. There were three branches in the vine. The vine began to bud then blossoms shot forth, then clusters of ripened grapes were brought forth before me. Pharaoh, the royal king of Egypt, his cup was in my hand. I took the ripened grapes and pressed them into Pharaoh's cup, then I put the cup into Pharaoh's hand. Joseph spoke to the chief butler of Pharaoh saying, this is the interpretation of it. The three branches represent three days. Within three days, the Pharaoh will lift your head up because he will restore you back to your place in his house. You will deliver Pharaoh's cup into his hand just as you use to when you were his chief butler.

When it becomes well with you, I hope you remember me and show me kindness. I hope you mention me to Pharaoh to bring me out of this dungeon. I have not done anything wrong, yet I was stolen away out of the land of my ancestors, out of the land that has been given to the Eberites (**Ay-vair**). Also, I have done nothing here to make them put me into Pharaoh's dungeon. When the chief baker saw that the interpretation was good, he spoke to Joseph saying, in my dream, I had three white baskets on my head. In the uppermost basket there was all manner of foods for Pharaoh, but the birds and insects did eat them out of the basket upon my head. Joseph answered saying, this is the interpretation of your dream. The three baskets represent three days. Within three days, the Pharaoh will lift up your head from off you. He will hang you on a tree, then the birds and insects will eat your flesh from off you. On the third day, it was the Pharaoh's birthday and he prepared a great feast. At that time, among his servants, the Pharaoh lifted up the head of the chief butler and the Pharaoh lifted the head up off of the chief baker. He restored the chief butler onto his butlership again, then the chief butler gave the Pharaoh his cup to drink. As Joseph had interpreted to them, the Pharaoh lifted the head off of the chief baker and hung his body on a tree. The chief butler did not remember Joseph. The chief butler forgot about him. At the end of two years, it came to pass, the Pharaoh (**Pair-oh**) had a prophetic dream. In the dream, the Pharaoh saw himself standing beside a river. Then, seven beautiful heifers came up out of the river. They were well fed and pleasant to the sight. Then, they went and started feeding in a meadow by the river. Pharaoh looked back at the river and seven different heifers came up out the river. These heifers were looked upon as evil and troublesome. These heifers were small and thin. They were not well fed. These heifers went and stood by the other heifers in the meadow close to the river. Then, the heifers that were looked upon as evil and troublesome devoured the seven heifers that were well fed and looked upon as beautiful. Then, I, Pharaoh awoke from this dream. I slept again and had a second dream. I looked and beheld seven ears of corn came up upon one corn stalk. These ears of corn were plump and firm. These seven ears of corn on the cornstalk looked very good. After them, I looked and I beheld a blast of the east wind, then seven very thin ears of corn sprung up. Then, the seven very thin ears of corn devoured the seven ears of corn that were plump and firm. Then, I, Pharaoh, awoke. I knew it was a dream. In the morning, my spirit was troubled and disturbed. I sent for all the magicians of Egypt. I invited all the astrologers, horoscopist, diviners, and wise men of Egypt. I, Pharaoh, told them my dream, but there was none that could understand. There was none that could interpret. Then, the chief butler spoke to the Pharaoh saying, to this day I remember my sin against Pharaoh. I remember the guilt that came from my sin. I remember my punishment for sinning against Pharaoh. I remember Pharaoh was very angry with his servants, therefore, he put me in his dungeon under the authority of the captain of the prison guard, me and the chief baker. We both dreamed a prophetic dream the same night, and we both need someone to interpret them according to each man's dream. There was a young man with us in the dungeon. He is an Eberite (**Ay-vair-ee**) and he served the captain of the prison guard. We told him our dreams and he understood them. He was able to interpret our dreams according to the dreams we had. It came to pass, it happened the same way he interpreted to us. You restored me back to my position and you hung the chief baker on a tree.

Then, Pharaoh sent for Joseph. They brought Joseph quickly out of the dungeon. Joseph shaved himself and changed his clothing, then came in to present himself before Pharaoh. Pharaoh spoke to Joseph saying, I have dreamed two prophetic dreams, and there is no one that understands. There is no one who can interpret them. I have listened to my butler. He told me that you understand prophetic dreams, and you can interpret them. Joseph answered Pharaoh saying, I am without the Eloheem. I am not a part of them. I am not a god, nor an angel, nor any godlike one of the Eloheem. The Eloheem will give Pharaoh an answer of peace. I am set apart from them, and their ways are not in me. Pharaoh responded to Joseph saying, in my dream, I looked at myself standing upon the edge bank of a river. Then, seven beautiful heifers came up out of the river. They were well fed and pleasant to the sight. Then, they went and started feeding in a meadow by the river. I, Pharaoh, looked back at the river and seven more heifers came up out the river. These heifers were small and thin. They were not well fed. These heifers were looked upon as evil and troublesome. Of this kind of wickedness and sorrow, I have never seen such as these in all the land of Egypt. These heifers that were looked upon as evil and troublesome devoured the first seven heifers that were beautiful and well fed. When the troublesome heifers had eaten up the well fed heifers, there was no way to tell they had eaten the well fed heifers because they still looked small and thin as they were at the beginning, then I awoke from this dream. I went to sleep again. I had another dream, in this dream, I looked and beheld seven ears of corn had come up upon one cornstalk. They were plump and firm. They looked very good. Then, after them, with the blast of the east wind, seven ears of corn that were thin and withered came up upon the cornstalk. The withered ears of corn devoured the seven good ears of corn. I told this to all the magicians, the astrologers, the horoscopist, diviners, and wise men of Egypt, but, no one could understand. No one could declare the meaning to me. Joseph responded to Pharaoh saying, the dream is prophetic, and both dreams are one in the same. The Almighty, the All Supreme Being, the All Supreme Ruler, the Creator of all things has showed Pharaoh what He is about to do. The seven good heifers represent seven years and the seven good ears of corn represent the same seven years. The prophetic dream is one and the same. Now, this is the matter that I have spoken to Pharaoh about. What the Almighty is about to do, He has showed to Pharaoh. There will be seven years of abundance. Seven years of plenty throughout all the land of Egypt. After those seven years of abundance, there will be seven years of famine. All the abundance will be forgotten in the land of Egypt because the famine will be very troublesome, and it will consume all the land. The Pharaoh had a double dream because this event has been set up and established by the Almighty and He will bring it to pass shortly. Now, let Pharaoh seek out a wise man who can think with intelligence. Let Pharaoh seek out a man who can consider, discern, and distinguish. Let Pharaoh set him over all the land of Egypt. In the seven years of abundance, let Pharaoh do this. Let Pharaoh allow this man to appoint officers over the land to keep the fifth part of the food in the land of Egypt. Let them gather all the food of those good years that come. Let them store up corn under the hand of Pharaoh and let them keep food in the cities. Let the food be stored for the land against the seven years of famine that will be in the land of Egypt so the land will not perish through the famine.

The things Joseph spoke were good in the eyes of Pharaoh and in the eyes of all his servants. Pharaoh spoke to his servants asking, where can we find a man as this one? Where can we find a man as this one who has the SPIRIT of the Almighty with him and upon him? Pharaoh spoke to Joseph saying, as much as the Almighty has shown you concerning all these things, there is no one so intelligent, discerning, and wise as you are. Now, you will oversee my house and its affairs. All my people will be ruled according to your word. Only by the throne will I be greater than you. Pharaoh chose and invited guests, then the Pharaoh proclaimed Joseph's authority, character, reputation, honor, and glory. Pharaoh continued speaking to Joseph saying, I am Pharaoh, no man will lift up his hand or foot without you in all the land of Egypt. The Pharaoh made Joseph bow down to his knee then Pharaoh made him ruler over all the land of Egypt, and people cried before him. Then, Pharaoh took the his signature ring from off his hand and put it on Joseph's hand, then clothed him with fine and precious garments. Pharaoh put a gold chain around Joseph's neck. Pharaoh called Joseph's name Zaphnathpaaneah (**Zaph-fin-nath-pah-nay-akh**). Pharaoh continued speaking to Joseph saying, see, I have established you to rule over all the land of Egypt. In the Pharaoh's chariot, Joseph rode in the second position, the position right after the Pharaoh. Joseph was thirty years old when he stood before Pharaoh, the royal king of Egypt. When Joseph went out from the presence of Pharaoh, he went throughout all the land of Egypt. Pharaoh gave Asenath (**Ah-sen-nath**), the daughter of Potipherah (**Po-tee-fer-rahk**), to be Joseph's wife. Potipherah was a priest of On (**Own**). On was a place of sun worship that bordered the land of Goshen. In the seven years of abundance, the earth brought forth food by the handfuls. According to what he told Pharaoh, Joseph gathered up all the food during the seven years of plenty, and he stored the food in the cities. He stored the food from the fields that was round about every city in the same manner. Joseph gathered a lot of corn in number. It was as much as the sand of the sea because the amount of corn he gathered could not be counted. Before the years of famine came Asenath, the daughter of Potipherah, the priest of On gave birth to two sons for Joseph. After the birth of his two sons, Joseph chose and invited guests. He spoke to them about the Almighty. He spoke to them saying, the Almighty, the All Supreme Being, the All Supreme Ruler has made me forget all my misery, all my sorrow, all my trouble, and all my father's house. Joseph brought his son before them and called his name Manasseh (**Mah-nah-sheh**). Joseph continued speaking to them saying, the Almighty has caused me to fruitful in the land of my affliction. Joseph brought his second son before them and called his name Ephraim (**Ef-rhye-eem**). Now, the seven years of abundance that was in the land of Egypt were ended. According to what Joseph had spoken, the seven years of famine began to come, and, the famine was in all lands, but in the land of Egypt, there was food. When all the land of Egypt was famished, the people cried to Pharaoh for food. Pharaoh spoke to all the Egyptians saying, go to Joseph, you do what he tells you to do. The famine was all over the surface of the Earth. Joseph opened all the storehouses. As the famine grew great in the land of Egypt, he sold food to the Egyptians. Then, all countries came into Egypt to buy food and corn from Joseph because the famine was very great in all lands. In a vision, Jacob saw corn in Egypt. He considered and discerned to see if he could respect what he had saw.

He advised himself on what he was caused to see, then he found joy in what had been revealed to him. When Jacob listened to a report be declared by a witness, he carefully considered and discerned. In the sight of others, Jacob saw his sons looking at one another, then Jacob spoke to his sons asking, why are you staring and gazing at one another? Jacob continued speaking to them saying, look, I have carefully considered and discerned what I have foreseen. I have carefully considered and discerned what I have heard. There is corn and food in Egypt. All you go there and buy food for us from there so we can live and not die before our time. Then Joseph's brothers went to buy corn and food in Egypt. Jacob did not send Joseph's brother Benjamin with his them because Jacob thought trouble might befall upon him. Among all those that came to buy food, the sons of Jacob were among them because the famine was very great in the land of Canaan. Joseph ruled the land with the power of a king and dominated the land like mighty warrior. It was him that sold food to all the people of the land. Now, Joseph's brothers had come and bowed themselves before him. Indeed, with their faces to the Earth, the bowed themselves before their brother Joseph. As foreseen, Joseph looked at his brothers present themselves before him, and he observed them. Joseph remembered the prophetic dreams that he had of them. Joseph knew they were his brothers, but his brothers did not recognize him. In the sight of others, as he was looking at their faces, he considered and advised himself. Joseph knew them, but he made himself appear as a foreigner to them. He made himself hard hearted, stubborn, and fierce. Joseph spoke roughly to them, asking them, where do you come from? They responded saying, we come from the land of Canaan to buy food. Joseph responded to them saying, you are spies. You want to expose the defenses of the land. You want to see if the land is undefended. They responded saying, no, these servants only want to buy food from the lord of the land. We are all the sons of the same man. We are men of good manners. We are honest and upright men. We are true men. These servants before you are no spies. Joseph responded to them saying, no, you have to come this land to expose its defenses. You want to see if this land is undefended. They responded back saying, these servants are twelve brothers. We are the sons of the same man in the land of Canaan, but this day, the youngest of us is with our father and one of our brothers is missing. Joseph spoke again saying, it is what I said it is, you are spies. You have come to this land to expose its defenses. You want to see if this land is undefended. Now, I will examine you, therefore, this is your trial. This is how you will prove to me you have good hearts. By the life of the Pharaoh, you will not leave this place except your youngest brother come here. One of you can go and get your youngest brother, but the rest of you will be kept in the dungeon. I will prove whether your words are true. I will see if there be any truth in you or else, by the life of Pharaoh, the royal king of Egypt, you are surely spies. Altogether, Joseph put them in the dungeon for three days. On the third day, Joseph spoke to them saying, the Eloheem, their angels, and godly ones fear me and I am a man of good morals. Do this, obey my command and live. If you are men of good manners, if you are honest and upright men, if you are true men, let one of your brothers be restrained in this dungeon, and the rest of you go, and carry corn and food for the famine of your houses. You will bring back your youngest brother to me, then you will have confirmed your words.

Therefore, you will not die before your time. The brothers did as Joseph commanded. Joseph's brothers spoke among themselves saying, we are very guilty concerning our brother. When he sought our favor, when he sought our mercy, we would not consider him. We observed the anguish of his soul. Now, because of it, this distress has come upon us. Reuben (**Reh-oo-vain**) responded to them saying, I told you not to sin against the child? You did not listen. You would not hear. You would not consider. Now, his blood is required of us. They did not know that Joseph understood them because he spoke to them by an interpreter. Joseph turn away from them and wept. Then, he returned to them again and continued conversing with them. Joseph took Simeon (**Shem-own**), and restrained him in front of their faces. Then Joseph commanded his men to fill their sacks with food and corn. Joseph also commanded his men to put every man's money back into his sack. Joseph commanded his men to give them food for their journey. This is what Joseph did for his brothers. They strapped their asses with the corn, then they departed away from there. At the inn for lodging, as one of them opened his sack to give his ass food, he noticed his money, he looked and beheld his money in the opening of the sack. He spoke to his brothers, saying, my money is restored. Another brother spoke saying, look, my money is restored in my sack also. They became afraid as their hearts grew faint. They spoke to one another asking, what is this that the Almighty has done to us? Now, they had come to the land of Canaan, and onto their father Jacob. They told him all that happened to them saying, the man who is the lord of the country is hard hearted, stubborn, and fierce. He spoke roughly to us. He believed us to be spies of the land. We responded to him saying, we are men of good manners. We are honest and upright men. We are true men. We are no spies. We are twelve brothers. We are sons of the same father. This day, one of our brothers is missing, and the youngest is with our father in the land of Canaan (**Ken-ah-an**). Then, the man, the lord of the country, spoke to us saying, leave one of your brothers here with me, then leave away to take food for the famine of your households. Then, bring your youngest brother back to me. This is how I will know you are true men. This is how I will know you are men of good manner. This is how I will know you are not spies, but indeed you are honest and upright men. Then, I will deliver your brother to you and you can trade and travel in the land. As the brothers emptied their sacks before Jacob, every man's money was in his sack. When they and their father saw the money, they became afraid. Their father Jacob spoke to them saying, Joseph is not here. Simeon is not here. Now, you will take Benjamin (**Ben-yah-meen**) away. You have robbed me of my children. In this matter, all these things are before me and against me. Reuben spoke to his father saying, if I do not bring Benjamin back to you, you can kill my two sons. Put Benjamin under my authority and I will bring him back to you again. Jacob responded to his son Reuben saying, my son Benjamin will not go there with you. His brother is dead and he is left alone. If trouble comes to him along the journey, then you will have brought me down into the grave from sorrow. Now, the famine was very massive and grievous in the land. When they had eaten up the corn they brought back from Egypt, their father told them to go again to buy themselves a little food. Judah reminded his father saying, the lord of the land solemnly protested against us. He told us that we will not see his face unless our youngest brother is with us.

Judah continued speaking to his father saying, we will go Egypt to buy food if you send our youngest brother with us. If you do not send him with us, then we will not go back to Egypt because the lord of the land told us we will not see his face unless our youngest brother is with us. Jacob responded saying, why do you deal worse with me? Why did you tell the lord of the land that you have other brothers? The brothers replied, the lord of the land demandingly asked us about our family. He asked us if our father is alive. He asked us if we have another brother. We told him according to his questions. How could we know that he would ask us to bring our youngest brother back with us? Judah spoke to his father saying, send the young boy with me, then we will go together so we can live and you, we, and our little ones will not die before our time. I will protect him so from my hand you can require him. If I do not bring him back to you and put him in front of you, then I will take the blame forever. Now, if we were not still lingering around her, by now we would have returned back there a second time. Jacob spoke to them saying, if it must be so. Now, do this. Get some of our best products, a little balm, a little honey, spices, myrrh, nuts, and almonds, then put them in your sacks. Carry them to that lord of the land for a gift. Take the money that was put back into your sacks, and take double that amount into your hand. Carry it back there with you just in case it was an oversight. Take your brother Benjamin with you and go back to the lord of that land. May the Almighty, the All Supreme Being, the All Supreme Ruler, the Creator of all things give you mercy in front of that lord of the land so he can give your other brother back to you along with Benjamin. If I lose my children, so be it, I am robbed of my children. Jacob's sons took the gift and double their money along with Benjamin and they went back to Egypt to stand in front of Joseph, the lord of the land. When Joseph saw Benjamin with them, he spoke to the servant over his house saying, bring these men to my home. Prepare food because these men will dine with me at noon time. The servant did as Joseph commanded. The man brought the brothers into Joseph's house. The brothers were afraid because they were brought into Joseph's house. They spoke to one another saying, we are brought here because of the money that was in our sacks from the first time. Now, he can charge us. Now, he can take us and our asses for slaves. They came near to the servant over Joseph's house. They conversed with him at the door. They spoke to him saying, o sir, we did come here the first time to buy food, but when we came to the inn for lodging, we opened our sacks. We saw that every man's money was in the opening of his sack, but we have brought it back to your hand. We cannot tell who put our money back in our sacks, but we have brought more money with us so we can buy food. Joseph's steward spoke to them saying, do not fear. The Almighty, you and your fathers' All Supreme Ruler has allowed treasure to be put in your sacks, then he brought Simeon out to be with them. Afterwards, the man brought the brothers into Joseph's house. He gave them water and they washed their feet. He gave their asses food also. They heard that they would eat food there at noon, so they prepared the present ahead of seeing Joseph. When Joseph came home, they brought their present into the house and gave it to him, then in front of him, they bowed themselves to the Earth. Joseph asked them about their welfare. He asked them if their father was still alive. He asked them if the old man they spoke about was doing well.

They bowed down their heads in respect, then they responded saying, our father is still alive and he is in good health. Joseph lifted up his eyes, then he saw his brother Benjamin. He asked them, is this your younger brother who you told me about? Joseph spoke again saying, the Almighty be gracious to you, my son. Now, Joseph became very emotional, and he moved quickly to find somewhere to weep. He entered into his chamber and wept there. After he stopped himself from crying, he washed his face and came out before them. He spoke to his servants saying, set out the bread and bring out the food. The servants set out food for Joseph by himself. The servants set out food for them by themselves. The Egyptians did not eat with Joseph because the Egyptians will not eat bread with Eberites (**Ay-vair-ee**) according to custom. It is wickedness to them. Indeed, the Egyptians may not eat bread with Eberites because that is considered an abomination. The brothers sat in front of Joseph. It was the firstborn according to his birthright then the youngest according to his youth. The men wondered with amazement at each other. Joseph took from his contributions and sent gifts to his brothers that were before him, but Benjamin's gift was five times as much as any of theirs. They drank with Joseph and they were very happy with him. Joseph commanded the steward of his house saying, fill these men's sacks with as much food as they can carry. Joseph commanded them to put every man's money back in his sack. Joseph commanded his steward saying, put my silver cup in the sack of the youngest along with his food and corn money. Joseph's steward obeyed his command and did according to what Joseph told him to do. As soon as the morning had light, Joseph's brothers were sent away along with their asses. Joseph commanded his steward saying, when they are gone out of the city and they have journeyed not far away, you get up and pursue those men. When you overtake them, you say this to them, why have you rewarded evil for good? Is this not the cup that my lord drinks from? Is this not the cup that my lord observes as an omen? Is this not the cup my lord uses to tell fortunes. You have committed evil by taking his cup. Joseph's steward obeyed him. He went to overtook them and he spoke Joseph's same words. Joseph's brothers responded saying, why has the lord of the land spoken these words? The ways of the Eloheem are far from us. The Almighty forbids His servants to do such things, therefore, it is far away from us to do according to this thing. Look and see, the money that we found in our sacks' opening, we brought that back to you. How could we steal silver or gold out of your lord's house? Whoever of us it is found with, let this man be put to death and we also will become the lord of the land's slaves. Joseph's steward responded saying, now, let it be according to these words, the man that the silver cup is found with will be Joseph's servant and the rest of you will be blameless. Then, every man took his sack down to the ground immediately and opened them. Joseph's servant searched. He began with the eldest and stopped at the youngest. The silver cup was found in Benjamin's sack. Then, the brothers began to tear their clothes from sorrow and every man tied their sack to their ass. They returned to the city in Egypt. Judah and his brothers came to Joseph's house. Joseph was still there and they fell onto the ground before him. Joseph spoke to them saying, why have you done this? What you do not know is that a man as I can certainly see the future. I can observe omens. I can foretell fortune. Judah spoke to Joseph asking, what can we say to the lord of the land?

How can we clear ourselves? The Almighty has searched and found sin among HIS servants. Now, we are all servants to the lord of this land. Joseph responded saying, the ways of the Eloheem are far away from me. The Almighty forbids me to do according to the thing you have spoken, but the man whose hand the cup has been found in, he will by my servant. As for the rest of you, you get up and go in peace to you father. Then, Judah came near to Joseph. Judah spoke to him saying, I pray that the lord of the land will let me speak a word in his ears. You are as Pharaoh. I pray you do not let your anger burn against this servant. You, the lord of the land, asked these servants saying, do you have a father or a brother? We responded to the lord of the land saying, yes, we have a father who is an old man and he had a child in his old age. Now this child's brother is dead, therefore, he is now the only son of his mother and his father loves him. You commanded us to bring him to you so you can look at him. We spoke to you, the lord of the land saying, this young boy cannot leave away from his father because if he should leave his father, his father would die before his time. You responded to us telling us, we will not see your face anymore except that our youngest brother is with us. When we came to my father, we told him the words that came from you, the lord of this land. Our father commanded us saying, go there again and buy us a little food. We responded saying, we cannot go back there except our youngest brother be with us, then we will go back because we cannot see the face of the lord of the land except our youngest brother be with us. My father spoke to us saying, you know that one of my wives gave birth to two sons for me. One of those sons departed away from me and I believe he is torn in pieces by a beast because I have not seen him since he departed away. If you take my other son from me, then trouble will befall upon him and you will bring my gray hairs along with my sorrow down to the grave with me. Now, seeing how my father's life is tied to this young boy's life, when I come before my father and this young boy is not with me, when my father sees that the young boy is not with us, he will die prematurely. Our father with his gray hair will go down into the grave from his sorrow. Concerning, this young boy, I gave my father assurance. I told him that if I do not bring him back to my father, then I will carry the blame forever. Now, I pray that you will let me stay instead of the young boy. I will be a slave to you, the lord of the land. Let the young boy go back to our father with his brothers. How can I go back in front of my father and the young boy is not with me? Unless I go back and see the evil that will come upon my father. Joseph could not restrain himself in front of all them that stood by him. He caused every servant that stood by him to leave away from his presence. Then, when no servant was standing beside him, he cried. Joseph made himself known to his brothers. As he wept aloud, the Egyptians and the house of Pharaoh paid attention to the sound of crying and they listened with interest. Joseph spoke to his brothers saying, I am Joseph. Is my father still living? His brothers could not answer him because they were nervous and very disturbed. Indeed, they were terrified at his presence. Joseph continued speaking to his brothers saying, I pray that you come near me, so they came near. Joseph spoke to them saying, I am your brother and I was sold into Egypt. Do not be grieved nor angry with yourselves that you gave me up to be sold here because the Almighty did send me here ahead of you to save lives. These two years the famine has been in the land, but there are five more years that will have no ploughing or harvest.

The Almighty sent me ahead of you because He has preserved you and saved the final portion of your descendants to be on the Earth. Now, it was not you nor the Eloheem that sent me here, but it was the Almighty. And, the Almighty has made me a prince to Pharaoh and I am lord of all his house. The ALMIGHTY has established me as a ruler throughout all the land of Egypt. Now, you go quickly. Go to my father and tell him this is what your son Joseph says, the Almighty has made me lord of all Egypt. Come here to be with me and do not wait. You will live in the land of Goshen (**Go-shen**), and you will live near me, you, your children, and your children's children, your flocks, your herds, and all that you have. There is another five years of famine and I will nourish you and all your household and all that you have. If you deny my request, you will come to misery and poverty. Joseph continued speaking to his brothers saying, look, you can see me with your eyes and the eyes of my brother Benjamin can see me. You all see that it is my mouth that speaks to you. You will tell my father about all my glory, all my abundance, all my honor, all my riches, and all my reputation in Egypt. You will tell him about all that you have witnessed. You will move quickly and bring my father to be with me. Joseph cried upon his brother Benjamin's neck and Benjamin wept upon his neck. Then, Joseph embraced and kissed all his brothers and wept upon them. After this, his brothers talked with him. Their sound was heard and became famous in Pharaoh's house. The servants of Pharaoh began proclaiming saying, Joseph's brothers have come here. This pleased Pharaoh and he thought good upon it. This pleased all the servants of Pharaoh and they thought well upon it. Pharaoh spoke to Joseph saying, tell your brothers to do this. Tell them to load their asses and get themselves into the land of Canaan. Get your father and all his household, then come back to me. I will give them the good of the land of Egypt, and, they will eat from the abundance in the land. Now, you have been commanded to do this. You will take wagons out of the land of Egypt to bring their little ones, their wives, and your father. Do not worry about their stuff because the good of all the land of Egypt is theirs. The sons of Jacob did so and Joseph gave them wagons according to the commandment that came from Pharaoh and for their journey Joseph gave them food according to their manner of living. He gave all of them clothing, but to Benjamin he gave three hundred pieces of silver and five changes of clothing. For the journey, Joseph sent ten asses loaded with the good things of Egypt to his father. For the journey, Joseph sent ten female asses loaded with corn, bread, and meat for his father according to his manner of living. Joseph spoke to his brothers saying, make sure you do not get lost on your journey nor turn away from your manner of living. Then, Joseph sent his brothers away and they departed. They left from out of Egypt and came into the land of Canaan and onto their father Jacob. The brothers spoke to their father saying, Joseph is still alive. He is lord over all the land of Egypt. Jacob's heart fainted because he did not believe them. They told him all the words Joseph spoke to them and when Jacob saw the wagons that Joseph had sent to carry him, Jacob's spirit was renewed. Jacob spoke to his sons saying, it is enough. My son Joseph is alive. I will go and see him before I die. Jacob took the journey with all that he had. He came to Beersheba (Bay-air-shah-bah). While he was there, he killed an animal and offered it as a sacrifice to honor the Almighty, the All Supreme Ruler of his father Isaac (**Yitz-hoc**). In the night, in a vision, the Almighty spoke to Jacob saying, Jacob. Jacob responded saying, I am here.

The Almighty replied saying, I am the ALMIGHTY, the ALL SUPREME BEING, the ALL SUPREME RULER, the CREATOR of all things. I am the All Supreme Ruler of your grandfather Abraham and of your father Isaac. Do not fear to go into Egypt because from there, I will make you become a great nation. I will go into Egypt with you. Joseph will put his hand upon your face and you will see him with your eyes. I will surely bring you back to the land I have given you. Jacob arose and departed away from Beersheba. The sons of Jacob carried their father, their little ones, and their wives in the wagons that Pharaoh had sent to carry them. They had their cattle and their goods that they had gotten in the land of Canaan, then Jacob and all his household came into Egypt together. Jacob entered Egypt with his sons, his grandsons, his daughters, his granddaughters, and all his children. These are the names of the children of Jacob that came into Egypt. It was Jacob's firstborn Reuben. The sons of Reuben were Hanoch (**Han-noak**), Phallu (**Pal-loo**), Hezron (**Hetz-roan**), and Carmi (**Care-mee**). Carmi is the progenitor of the Carmites. The sons of Simeon were Jemuel (**Yeh-moo-ale**), Jamin (**Yah-meen**). Jamin is the progenitor of the Jamites. There was Ohad (**O-had**), then Jachin (**Yah-heem**). Jachin is the progenitor of the Jachinites. There was Zohar (**Tso-hare**), then Shaul (**Shah-ool**). Shaul was the son of a Canaanitish woman. The sons of Levi (**Lay-vee**) were Gershon (**Gair-shown**), then Kohath (**Kay-hath**), then Merari (**Meh-rah-ree**). The sons of Judah (**Yeh-who-dah**) were Er (**Air**), then Onan (**O-nawn**), but as a penalty of neglecting wise conduct and good morals, Er and Onan died prematurely in the land of Canaan. They were put to death by magician warlocks of necromancy. The third son of Judah was Shelah (**Sheh-lah**), then Pharez (**Pair-retz**), and Zerah (**Zeh-rahk**). Pharez and Zerah were twin brothers. The sons of Pharez were Hezron (**Hetz-roan**) and Hamul (**Hah-mool**). The sons of Isaachar (**Yis-sahs-har**) were Tola (**Toe-lah**). Tola is the progenitor of the Tolaites. There was Phuvah (**Pu-ah**), then Job (**Yove**), and Shimron (**Shem-roan**). Shimron is the progenitor of the Shimronites. The sons of Zebulun (**Zev-voo-loon**) were Sered (**Seh-red**), then Elon (**Ay-loan**), then Jahleel (**Yahk-lah-ale**). Jahleel is the progenitor of the Jahleelites. The sons of Gad (**God**) were Ziphion (**Zef-fone**). Ziphion is the progenitor of the Zephonites. There was Haggi (**Hag-gee**). Haggi is the progenitor of the Haggites. There was Shuni (**Shu-nee**). Shuni is the progenitor of the Shunites. There was Ezbon (**Es-voan**), then Eri (**Air-ree**). Eri is the progenitor of the Erites. There was Arodi (**Air-rode**). Arodi is the progenitor of the Arodites. There was Areli (**Air-ay-lee**). Areli is the progenitor of the Arelites. The sons of Asher (**Ah-share**) were Jimnah (**Yim-nah**), then Ishuah (**Yish-vah**), then Isui (**Ish-vee**). Isui is the progenitor of the Ishuaites. There was Beriah (**Bear-ree-yah**). Then, their sister Serah (**Say-rahk**). The sons of Beriah were Heber (**Hev-vair**). Heber is the progenitor of the Heberites. There was Malchiel (**Mal-kee-ale**). The sons of Joseph were Manasseh (**Mah-nay-sheh**) and Ephraim (**Ef-rhye-eem**). The sons of Benjamin were Belah (**Bah-lyh**), then Becher (**Bahk-her**), then Ashbel (**Ash-bel**), then Gera (**Gay-rah**). Naaman (**Nah-ah-mon**) was the son of Belah. There was Ehi (**Ay-hee**), then Rosh (**Rosh**), then Muppim (**Mah-peem**), then Huppim (**Hah-peem**), and Ard (**Aird**). Dan (**Don**) had one son named Hushim (**Ho-sheem**). The sons of Naphtali (**Naph-tah-lee**) were Jahzeel (**Yahk-zah-ale**). Jahzeel is the progenitor of the Jahzeelites.

There was Guni (**Goo-nee**). Guni is the progenitor of the Gunites. There was Jezer (**Yates-zair**). Jezer is the progenitor of the Jezerites. There was Shillem (**Shah-lame**). These are all the souls that came with Jacob into the land of Egypt. Now, Jacob sent Judah ahead of him to meet Joseph for to direct him to Goshen. Jacob and all his household came into the land of Goshen. Joseph prepared his chariot, then went to meet his father Jacob in Goshen. Joseph presented himself to his father, then embraced him, and cried on his neck a long time. Jacob spoke to Joseph saying, because you are still alive and I have seen your face, now I can die. Joseph spoke to his brothers and to every one of his father's household, saying, I will go up to Pharaoh and make it known. I will declare to him that my brothers and every one of my father Jacob's household that were in the land of Canaan have come to me. Then, they will publish and announce the report. I will tell him our men are shepherds and their trade has been to feed cattle, therefore, they have brought their flocks, their herds, and all that they have. When Pharaoh chooses and invites to you speak to him, he will ask, what is your occupation? You will say, from our youth even until now, our trade has been about cattle: we, our father, our father's father, and so on. Because every shepherd is an abomination to the Egyptians, you will say this so you can live in the land of Goshen. Then Joseph spoke to Pharaoh saying, my father, my brothers, my brethren, their flocks, their herds, and all they possess have come out of the land of Canaan. Now, they are in the land of Goshen. Joseph chose five men out of his brethren and presented them before Pharaoh. Pharaoh spoke to them asking, what is your occupation? They responded saying, we are shepherds, so is our father, so was our father's father, and so on. For the food and corn that was being bought, Joseph gathered up all the money that was to be found in the land of Egypt and also in the land of Canaan, then Joseph brought the money into Pharaoh's house. When the money failed in the land of Egypt and in the land of Canaan, all the Egyptians came to Joseph. They spoke to Joseph saying, the money has failed. Give us food and bread. Why should we die in your presence? Joseph spoke to them saying, if your money has failed, give me your cattle, and I will give you food and bread. They brought their cattle to Joseph. Joseph gave them food and bread in exchange for their horses, their flocks, their asses, and their herds of cattle. That year, Joseph fed them with food and bread for all their cattle. When that year had ended, they came to Joseph the second year. They spoke to him saying, how our money was spent, we cannot hide it from the lord of the land. The lord of the land has our herds of cattle. Now, in the sight of the lord of the land, there is nothing left to give except our bodies and our lands. Therefore, will we die before your eyes, both us and our land? For food and bread buy us, then we and our land will be servants to Pharaoh. Give us seed to sow in the ground so we can live and not die, so the land is not empty. Joseph bought all their land for Egypt. These persons sold their fields because the famine triumphed over them, therefore, the land now belonged to Pharaoh. As for the people of the fields, he moved them to cities from one end of the Egyptian border to the other. Only the land of the priests he did not buy because the priest had a portion assigned to them by Pharaoh. They did eat their portion that Pharaoh gave them, therefore, they did not sell their lands. Joseph spoke to the people saying, this day I have purchased you and your land for Pharaoh.

ow, here is seed for you and you will be able to sow in the land. When your seed increases, you will give a fifth of it to Pharaoh and four parts will be your own. Four parts will be for your own food to feed them of your households and to sow seed in the field. They responded saying, because you have save our lives, we will be Pharaoh's servants, but let us find favor and acceptance in the sight of the lord of the land. To this day, it is a law that Joseph made over the land of Egypt that Pharaoh will have the fifth part except for the land of the priests which doesn't belong to Pharaoh. Jacob lived in the land of Egypt, in the country of Goshen. He and his household had possessions and they and their possessions grew and multiplied greatly. Jacob lived in the land of Egypt seventeen years. The complete age of Jacob was one hundred forty-seven years. As the time drew near for Jacob to die, he called for his son Joseph. Jacob spoke to Joseph saying, now if I have found favor and acceptance in your sight, put your hand on top of my thigh and I pray that you will deal truthfully and kindly with me. I pray that you do not bury me in Egypt. You will carry me out of Egypt and bury me in the burying place of my father and his father. Joseph responded saying, I will do as you have requested. Jacob responded saying, take an oath to me. Joseph took an oath to honor his father Jacob. Jacob stretched himself out upon the bed. After these things, someone told Joseph that his father Jacob was very sick. Joseph took his two sons Manasseh (**Men-nay-sheh**) and Ephraim (**Ef-ryhe-eem**) with him. Someone told Jacob that his son Joseph was coming to him. Jacob encouraged himself and strengthened himself as he sat upon his bed. Jacob spoke to Joseph saying, the Almighty has observed me. He has given His attention to me. He has considered and approved of me. He has respected me and looked upon me with joy. In the sight of others, HE has provided for me. The Almighty has caused me be congratulated, praised, and adored in the sight of others. In the land of Canaan, outside the city of Luz (**Looz**), at **Bayith Shah-dye**, in a vision, the Almighty appeared to me. He presented Himself and looked at me in my face. Then, He caused me to foresee. In the vision, He promised me. He spoke to me saying, I will make you fruitful and I will multiply you to become numerous. I will make a multitude of people come from you. I will give this land to your children, to your children's children, to your children's posterity, and of your posterity, to your descendants who are of moral quality and of them to a practitioner of righteousness. I will give this land to them for an everlasting possession. Now, for Reuben and Simeon, your two sons, Ephraim and Manasseh, who were born to you in the land of Egypt before I came are mine, indeed, for Reuben and Simeon, your two sons are now mine. There is an issue of them being born after you left your native country, nevertheless, they are of my lineage, therefore, they will be chosen and summoned with the same name as their brethren in their inheritance. As for me, when I came from Padan, as we were journeying in the land of Canaan, Rachel died beside me when there was but a little ways to go to get to Ephrath. She lived according to our customs. She died living according to our customs. Jacob looked at Joseph's sons and asked, who are these? Joseph responded to his father saying, they are my sons whom the Almighty has given me in this place. Jacob spoke saying, I pray that you bring them to me and I will bless them to be praised and adored. Now the eyes of Jacob were weak and dim from old age, therefore, he could not see well.

Joseph embraced and kissed his sons, then brought them near to his father Jacob. Jacob spoke to Joseph saying, I did not think I would see your face again, but look and see, the Almighty has showed me your children also. Joseph brought them out from between his knees, then he bowed himself with his face toward the earth. With Ephraim in Joseph's right hand toward Jacob's left hand, with Manasseh in Joseph's left hand toward Jacob's right hand, Joseph brought them near to his father Jacob. Wittingly guiding his hands, Jacob stretched out his right hand and laid it upon Ephraim's head. Ephraim was the younger of Joseph's two sons. Jacob stretched out his left hand and laid it upon Manasseh's head. Manasseh was Joseph's firstborn. Jacob blessed Joseph and spoke saying the Almighty, the All Supreme Being, the All Supreme Ruler, whose ways my grandfather Abraham, and my father Isaac did live according to and who is the same All Supreme Ruler that has fed me all my long life to this day. The Almighty who redeemed me from all evil bless these two young boys to be congratulated, praised, and adored. Let my name be named onto them. Let the name of my grandfather Abraham and let the name of my father Isaac be named onto them. Let them grow to become numerous. Let them grow into a multitude of people that live upon the Earth. When Joseph saw that his father's right hand was upon the head of Ephraim, it displeased him. Joseph held up his father's hand to remove it from Ephraim's head and put it upon Manasseh's head. Joseph spoke to his father saying, not so father, put your right hand upon the head of my firstborn. Jacob refused saying, I know it my son. I know it. Your firstborn will become a multitude of people also. He will be great but truly, his younger brother will be greater than he and his offspring will become a multitude of people and a multitude of nations. Jacob blessed them that day saying, joined to you Joseph, the house of Jacob will be blessed, then Jacob put Ephraim before Manasseh. Jacob spoke to Joseph saying, I am dying, but the Almighty will be with you and He will bring you back to the land of your fathers. Moreover, I have given you one portion above your brethren, I am giving you that which I took out of the hand of the Amorite with my sword and my bow. Jacob summoned his sons. He summoned them to talk to them. He spoke to them saying, gather yourselves together to me so I can tell you the future. Assemble yourselves to me so I can tell you what will happen to your descendants at the end time. I will tell you what will happen to your remnant of people at the end of the whole age. In the day of trouble, in the day of troubled weather, at the last event, for the final issue, I will tell you what will be caused to happen and the reward that the Almighty will give to the residue of your descendants. Now, gather yourselves together and listen with interest. You sons of Jacob pay attention to your father. Give your ears to listen to your father Jacob. Jacob spoke to them saying, the Almighty, the All Supreme Being, the All Supreme Ruler, the Creator of all things has observed me. He has given his attention to me. He has considered and approved of me. He has respected me and looked upon me with joy. In the sight of others, the Almighty has provided abundantly for me. The Almighty has caused me be congratulated, praised, and adored in the sight of others. In the land of Canaan, outside the city of Luz (**Looz**), at **Bayith Shah-dye**, in a vision, the Almighty appeared to me. He presented Himself to me and looked at me in my face. Then, He caused me to foresee. In the vision, He promised me.

He spoke to me saying, I will make you fruitful and I will multiply you to become numerous. I will make a multitude of people come from you. I will give this land to your children, to your children's children, to your children's posterity, and of your posterity, to your descendants who are of moral quality and with them to a practitioner of righteousness. I will give this land to them for an everlasting possession. At, Penuel (**Pen-oo-ale**), the Angel of the Eloheem declared onto me. He promised me the reputation, the character, the authority, the glory, the honor, and the name of Israel, then that angel of the Eloheem congratulated me and praised me in adoration. Reuben, you are my firstborn. Of man and woman, you are my eldest son. You are powerful as the Eloheem. You have strength as those angels who are of man and behemoth. You have the ability to change as the chameleon, but you are of my strength and my health. In order and rank, you are the first from my ability to produce wealth and success. You have accepted the excellency of being superior. You have accepted the excellency of being proud in character, therefore, you are left with self-rising dignity and self-exaltation. You will remain in the excellence of superiority and you will rest with those that come up of animals, who have plenty, who are harsh, fierce, strong, and greedy for power. You lust recklessly. Your speech is of froth, therefore, your talk is worthless. You have wasted your semen, therefore, you are as piss that washes away with the water. You are dangerous, violent, and unstable. You went into your father's bedchamber and laid down on his bed and had sexual contact. You have disrespected the reputation and authority of the Covenant that comes from the Almighty. You have violated the honor of the Covenant and the

Commandment that comes from the Almighty. You have polluted your father's bed by having sex with his wife. Then, you went upon your father's couch and laid down on his couch and had sexual contact with his wife. You have treated the Almighty's Covenant and Commandment as a common thing. You have ritually polluted yourself and dishonored the Covenant and the Commandment. You will not be given the abundance saved over for the remnant of your father's family. You have killed your remnant's inheritance and it will not be restored. You will not have a remnant of people saved over. You will not have a remnant of people left over to remain and excel. Simeon and Levi are brothers that have dubious morals that cannot be relied on. In their habitations, there is equipment for hunting and war, in their habitations, there are utensils, tools, music, and objects for hunting and war. In their habitations, there are stabbing swords and stabbing devices. They have instruments of the oppressor, instruments of cruelty, and violence in their habitations. They have equipment and instruments for doing wrong and dealing violently. My soul is a living being within the blood of my body and is a ghost with an activity of mind and an activity of will. My soul is a living being within the blood of my body and is with emotions, appetites, passions, and characteristics as a beast, an animal, or creature. My mind or body has not desired to be brought into their secret counsel nor their intimate sessions with the Eloheem, therefore, do not go into their secret circle of friends. Do not desire nor be brought into their assemblies for evil counsel that are of war, invasion, and their religion of returning exiles. My tablets of inscription is not the same as theirs. The weight of my honor, my dignity, my glory, my reputation, my reverence, and my abundance is not the same as theirs.

My tablets of inscription are not joined to theirs nor are they united with theirs. The weight of my honor, my dignity, my glory, my reputation, my reverence, and my abundance is not joined; nor is it united with theirs. They murdered a great man of high degree who was a servant of mankind. They attacked him with deadly intent and with their hands; they killed him, then made a slaughter of his people. For their own pleasure and delight, for their own desire and goodwill, they voluntarily traveled about the city's wall exterminating its people and cattle. They showed great stubbornness. Their anger was outpouring with passion, and outpouring with arrogance, with fierceness, and with greediness. Their anger was overflowing with rage and fury. Their anger was cruel and severe. It caused severe grief. It caused severe burden. The Almighty will cast them abroad and scatter them into the household of Israel, who is Jacob, according to the angel of the Eloheem at Penuel (**Pen-oo-ale**). The Almighty will break them to pieces. The Almighty will plunder them and will take away their portion of inheritance. He will assign and distribute their portion among the household of Jacob. The Almighty loathes their passion for anger. The Almighty has put a bitter curse on their passion for anger. He has laid a bitter curse on the person that is passionate for anger. Therefore, the person that is passionate for anger will be made to be a bitter curse that is loathing. Judah, you are him whom your brothers, your relatives, and those like your brothers will honor and give thanks for. You are him whom they will confess their sin to and you are him whom they will confess the honor, the reputation, the character, the glory, and the authority of the Almighty to. You are him whom your brethren and those like your brethren will revere. Your strength, your power, and your hands will be joined to the neck of those of apostasy who have turned their back against the Almighty. Your hands will be joined to the neck of those that are stubborn against the Almighty. Your hands will be joined to the neck of those that are your adversaries. Your power and your strength will be against those that are your personal enemies, against those that are your nation's enemies, and against those that hate you. Your father's children's descendants will pay homage to you because you are him whom the royalty of the Almighty belongs to. Your father's children's descendants will humbly bow down before you. My son Judah's people are sent onto the stranger to be afflicted and there is one born in servitude of the stranger. My son Judah's descendant is an anointed child that will come up among the common rebels and robbers. The adversary Baal, lord of dreams, his king, his lords, his men with vision, and his archers grieve him greatly. They shoot arrows at him and they hate him. The citizens that are confederate and the persons that have sworn themselves to Baal and his king have grieved him greatly. The babbling bird has annoyed him, frustrated him, and worried him with things that are of no value. Altogether, they have dealt with him bitterly. They have frustrated him, annoyed him, and worried him with things that are not important. They have used their strength to provoke him to be angry and bitter. Altogether, they bear a grudge against him. Altogether, they retain animosity against him and cherish their animosity against him. In their hate, they lurked, laid snares, and followed him closely to persecute him, provoke him, and cause him to be enraged in his own bitterness.

He was feeble and in his weakness, he was struck until he was cast down and subdued. He was brought very low and in reverence, he kneeled down and bowed himself over to be in the rest of animals. But, his might is of the Covenant of the rainbow. His might has been set to endure and will be caused to be permanent by the ever flowing strength, by the ever flowing power of the Almighty, the All Supreme Being, the King of kings, the Creator of all things. The Almighty, the All Supreme Ruler of your chief ancestor and forefathers will help him. The Almighty will support him, give him aid, and surround him with His defense. The blessing that is on the head of Joseph, who began as an untrimmed vine, who was separated from his brothers by a band of men, and was poor among every man, then by the highest ruler, whose height is of the stars, Joseph was declared to be a sacred ruler of all the people and places of his time. Joseph was declared into the highest part of rulership. These blessings of Joseph is on the crown of the head of him, the Almighty's Devoted One, who is as an untrimmed vine, who has been separated from his brethren, and is poor among every man. He is to be declared the Holy Prince. The Almighty will summon him to His own Heaven, the highest heaven. He will kneel before the Almighty, and be blessed generously by the Almighty Himself. The Almighty will bless him abundantly, to be greatly congratulated, to be greatly praised, and to be greatly adored. At the end of the ceremony, he will be presented with a gift, and his blessings will be bestowed upon him. By the blessing of the Almighty, he will be blessed with the treaty of peace, he will become a source of blessings and a source of prosperity. The Almighty literally becomes His FATHER and His immediate family. My son Judah's descendant is of the Almighty's royalty, a member of the Almighty's own household. He is the first and only of his class of person. He will be blessed with the prosperity of the deep sea and of the deep places that are laid out under the heaven above. He will be praised and adore by women of breasts who carry the womb. He will have compassion and mercy for men and women. Indeed, He will receive the highest blessing and He will be the praise of the Almighty. For a man to become a source of blessing, a source of prosperity, a source of peace, and to become the praise of the Almighty with the blessings of kingship, respect, and honor; these blessings have prevailed above the blessings, the peace, and prosperity given to my progenitors. The Almighty has given him stronger, mightier, prouder, and greater blessings than the blessings given to my progenitors. Therefore, the blessings of His Father, who is the Almighty has fixed what has been broken. The blessings given to him from his Father, the Almighty, will always be confirmed, will always be strong, will always be powerful, will always be proud, and will always be mighty to the full extent of eternity, to the full limit of everlasting. For a sign, for a monument, and for remembrance, his strength will forever remain mighty to keep custody of the Law, to keep order of the Law, to keep the labor, the work, and the service of the Law, to keep the fellowship of the Law, to keep the land of the Law, and to keep dominion. The strength and power of his military and political forces are made solid and strong, and, is bound to the ever flowing power of the Almighty, the All Supreme Being, the All Supreme Ruler of your father Jacob. His forces are made to be fast, agile, and they are bound to the power of the Almighty.

His forces are mighty in power and stretch their arms out to help. My son Judah's descendant is found worthy and is appointed to be Steward to a family of mighty people. My son Judah's descendant is the firstborn son of the Almighty. He is the first of his kind, the first of his class, and the first and only of his condition. From this, by the Eloheem, comes the shepherd of idolatry, who is a ruler, a teacher, and a special friend of the people that cares for the people. This is the shepherd of idolatry and is called the stone of Israel. At the Judgment of the Almighty, the stars will fade. At the break of day at dawn, my son Judah's descendant will be carried away ascending up as a natural phenomenon. He will come up before the Almighty, the All Supreme Being, the All Supreme Ruler, the Creator of all things. The Almighty will recover him and restore him. The Devoted One will grow over and be made superior. He will be exalted and made to excel. He will be mentally stirred up and brought against those that come up of animals. He will cut off those that come up of animals, and those that have remained in an animal condition. He washed his garments with the blood of his enemies and his clothes are as the treading down on clusters of grapes. Bound with cord to his colt, he takes his prisoners of war to the house of Jacob and to the nobles of the house of Jacob. His mental abilities and spiritual faculties will be intoxicating as banqueting with wine. His knowledge, his countenance, and his presence will be intoxicating as banqueting with wine. His face and outward appearance will be made very well and his humbleness will be intoxicating as banqueting with wine. His teeth are the teeth of a man, white as ivory, white as milk. He will set up the justice and work of the Almighty. Imagine a young fierce lion, now picture this violent young lion is abroad tearing the prey into pieces, then he is caused to lay down and rest. Imagine that same young lion becoming a great and powerful lion, violent, and fierce laying down resting. What enemy will come on the scene to establish themselves? What enemy will arise to attack and succeed? What enemy could endure? My son Judah's descendants will be carried away ascending up as a natural phenomenon. They will come up before the Almighty, the All Supreme Being, the All Supreme Ruler, the Creator of all things. The Almighty will recover them and restore them. They will grow over and be made superior. They will be exalted and made to excel. They will be mentally stirred up and brought against those that come up of animals. They will cut off those that come up of animals and those that remain in an animal condition. They will set up and establish the justice of the Almighty. They will set up and establish the work of the Almighty. Imagine young mighty and fierce lions, now picture these violent young lions are abroad tearing the prey into pieces, then they are caused to lay down and rest. What enemy will come on the scene to establish themselves? What enemy will arise to attack and succeed? What enemy could endure? Judah is the family of the scepter with the mark of authority and the scepter will not be removed to and from Judah. The scepter with the mark of authority will not be taken away from Judah by rebels. The scepter with the mark of authority will not be caused to reject Judah nor turn aside from Judah. According to the time of the journey and its pace on broken feet, according to the possessions of the journey, according to the haunting of the journey, no lawgiver or no scribe can endure tracing and marking out ancient inscriptions of print that was appointed to the scribes and lawgivers until Shiloh (**Shee-low**) is caused to come and be introduced.

No lawgiver or scribe can endure tracing and marking out the traces of the appointed ancient law that was prescribed to scribes and lawgivers until Shiloh (**Shee-low**) is caused to come and be introduced. According to the time of the journey and its pace on broken feet, according to the possessions of the journey, according to the haunting of the journey, no scribe can endure hacking ancient inscriptions of print, marking out the roles of animals, of Seraphim, of Cheribum, and the idols of the scribes and lawgivers. No lawgiver or scribe can endure the journey to portray the violent encounters of the lawgivers and scribes that have been cut in, cut on, and cut out until Shiloh comes. All these things are what belongs to him or whose it is. Peace and rest belongs to him. After Shiloh's coming, the people of the nations will be purged and cleansed, then they will gather onto Shiloh and obey him. Zebulun will live in covered habitations by the seashore. He will be a sheltered habitation for seamen, and ships of men on the coast of the sea. His border will be onto Zidon (**See-doan**). Between the fireplaces, and heaps of ash, lurking and crouching down between two sheepfolds, Issachar is a strong-boned body sitting between two burdens. He was caused to see the resting place. When the resting place appeared, he looked at the condition of the resting place and considered. He observed the quietness, the peacefulness, and the comfortableness of that resting place, then he saw it become better. He observed the ground, the inhabitants and the cities of the resting place. He discerned, He distinguished, then he advised himself. He advised himself that the resting place was beautiful and excellent of its kind. He advised himself the resting place was the best benefit for his welfare, happiness, and prosperity. He advised himself the inhabitants of the land were happy, beautiful, and pleasant. He advised himself the inhabitants of the land were with good people of understanding, good morals, and good ethics. He was enticed and became a servant and worshipper of the Almighty. He offered his strength and his back to help carry the burden. He is caused to be a taskmaster over the labor for the slaves. He oversaw the task workers that forced slaves to tribute by doing labor, he enlisted task workers to force slaves to tribute by doing labor, and he oversaw the liberation of slaves forced to tribute by doing labor. Dan will make great efforts of quarrel with his people. He will judge his people and kinsman. He will contend with his people and kindred. He will be at strife with his people and kinsman. He will become a tribe of Israel, the name given to your father Jacob by an angel of the Eloheem at Peniel. Imagine you are journeying on your way to collect an inheritance and a serpent is thrown in the path near to where you are journeying. Now, the serpent is lying in wait to attack. The serpent hisses at your footsteps, then bites your heels from behind. As a result, you fall a violent death and you lose your inheritance. Now, your inheritance will be divided by lot. Now, picture an adder that is thrown in the road on the same path of a traveler moving on a swift horse. The rider is on his way to collect his inheritance. The adder is lying in wait to attack. At the horse's hoofs, that serpent hisses then bites the horse's heels from behind so that the rider who is mounted on the horse is caused to fall off. The rider is thrown down and fall a violent death. The rider will be stretched out dead. He would lose his inheritance and it would be divided by lot. Dan will be an enchanter, practicing fortune telling, observing signs, omens, and whispering spells.

Divination will be the habits of his life and the course of his life. His custom of conversation will be about fortune telling, omens, and divination. In the time to come, at the hinder part, Dan will be judged. He will be thrown down and fall a violent death. He will lose his inheritance and it will be divided by lot. Gad, a troop of strangers will crowd upon you. Gad, a troop of robbers will attack and invade your habitation. They will overcome Gad, but at the last part, at the hinder part, Gad will crowd upon the enemy. He will attack and invade them. Indeed, Gad will overcome those that lie in wait. The food, the fruit, and the bread of Asher will be plentiful. His food will be healthy, rich in flavor, and rich in smell. He will be given wages to sell and exchange his delicacies. He will be considered and assigned to produce the consecrated food and delicacies for the Royal King. Naphtali is like a deer let go and pushed away to be set free. He is ordained to publish beautiful and elegant words that are of the Promise and Commandment of the Almighty. It is appointed to him to speak goodness and goodliness. He will be entrusted to deliver good words and beautiful words. His elegant sayings and elegant words will be published. He will be paid wages to speak and he will be permitted to sell and exchange his publications for wages. Joseph is a fruitful son that has shown mental qualities and spiritual faculties. Joseph 's looks good in the face and well in his outward appearance. With a humble presence, Joseph is a fruitful son and he is caused to bring forth daughters born of servitude under the hands of the stranger. They came up among the rebel and robber. Joseph's daughters, their female cousins, and all those girls that are related to them will become the first of their kind.

They are women of mental qualities and spiritual faculties. They look good in the face and well in their outward appearance. They are polite, considerate, humble, and very fruitful. They are a mighty company of women. They step and march in stride to the same pace. They will surround the walls that house the harlot and they will push down the walls that house the harlot. They will surround the walls that house the harlot and run through and over the walls that house the harlot. They are swift, with strength, they are able to spring and leap about. They will surround the walls that house the rich and they will push down the walls that house the rich. They will surround the walls that house the rich and they will run through and over the walls that house the rich. Like a frightening wolf tearing its prey into pieces and providing food from what has been torn in pieces, at the end of night, at the break of day, at the coming of daylight, Benjamin will eat and devour plenty of the prey. His aim is to attack and destroy the prey. He will freely kill with the sword. With fire, he will burn up the things that do not move. Then, in the night, he will assign and distribute the plunder of the war. He will receive his portion of the spoil and share the remaining portion of the spoil. These are all the sons of Jacob. This is what their father spoke to them about, then he blessed them to be congratulated, saluted, praised, and adored. Jacob blessed his sons, every one of them according to his blessing. Jacob charged his sons and command them saying, I am to be brought to the land of my fathers, and there my people will assemble and gather to me. Bury me in the land of Canaan, in the field of Machpelah.

Bury me with my grandfather Abraham and my father Isaac in the cave that is in the field of Machpelah. The cave that my grandfather Abraham bought from Ephron (**Eff-roan**), the Hittite (**Haith**) for possession of a burial place. There, they buried my grandfather Abraham and his wife Sarah (**Sah-rah**). There, they buried my father Isaac (**Yitz-hoc**) and his wife Rebekah (**Rev-kah**). There, I buried my wife Leah (**Lay-ah**). When Jacob had made an end of commanding his sons, he put his feet up into the bed. As he was about to die, he took his last breath, then his soul departed, and his body died. Joseph accepted judgment and his portion of the inheritance. Joseph accepted his father's death. He accepted all his father's household. Joseph accepted to honor and respect the Almighty, the All Supreme Ruler of his forefathers, of his grandfather, and of his father. From fear and from heaviness, in the presence of his family, in front of all their faces, Joseph fell upon his father's face. In grief, he cried. He wept bitterly over his father Jacob. As he was lamenting, he gently touched his father and kissed him upon his face. Joseph commanded his servant physicians to embalm his father Jacob with ripen spices and with ripened spices, the physicians embalmed. Forty days of mourning were completed for Jacob. This is the same time of days given to those who are embalmed, but the Egyptians mourned Jacob for eighty days. When the days of his mourning Jacob had passed, Joseph spoke to the house of Pharaoh saying, now, if I have found acceptance and favor in your sight, I pray that you will speak in the ears of Pharaoh, tell him, my father Jacob made me take an oath saying, he will be buried in the grave that has been dug for him in the land of Canaan. Now, this is where I must bury him. Pharaoh responded saying, go to Canaan. Bury your father according to the oath you took to honor him. Joseph departed away and went to Canaan to bury his father Jacob. The servants of Pharaoh, elders of his house, and all elders of the land of Egypt were with Joseph as he journeyed to Canaan to bury his father. All the house of Joseph, his brethren, all of Jacob's house went with Joseph to bury Jacob in the land of Canaan. They left their flocks, their herds, and their children in the land of Goshen. It was a very great company of people. Both chariots and horsemen traveled with Joseph to Canaan to bury his father Jacob. They journeyed to an area across and beyond the Jordan (**Yair-dain**). Then they came to an open area, an empty place that had thorn trees. They had come to a place called Atad (**Ah-tahd**). There, they mourned with a very heavy and great lamentation. For seven days, Joseph set up a mourning for his father Jacob. When the inhabitants of the land, the Canaanites, saw a mourning set up in the open area of Atad, they spoke to themselves saying, this mourning is moving slow and it is massive. The Egyptians are numerous in number. So, the name of it was called Abelmizraim (**Av-vail-mitz-rhy-eem**), meaning the meadow of Egypt. Jacob's sons respected him as an honorable man, they would spare anything to help him. His sons did according to what he commanded, and brought him into the land of Canaan to be buried with his fathers. They buried him in the cave of the field of Machpelah. Abraham bought this field and cave for a possession of a burying place. He purchased it from Ephron, the Hittite. After he buried his father, Joseph returned into Egypt; he, his brethren, and all those who went into the land of Canaan with him to bury his father. When Joseph's brothers considered and discerned that their father was dead.

They presented themselves one to another. They look at each other in the face and spoke to one another saying, now Joseph will be hostile toward us. He will turn away from the Almighty. He will hate us as an enemy. He will bring back all the evil upon us that we have did to him. He will lead us away and bring distress upon us. They sent a messenger to Joseph. They told the messenger to say this saying, before your father died, he commanded you and prayed that you would forgive your brothers of their trespass. He commanded you and prayed that you will forgive their sin. Your brothers did deal evilly with you. Now, forgive your brethren who are fellow servants and worshippers of the Almighty. When Joseph heard the message from his brothers, he cried. Then Joseph's brothers came to him presenting themselves. They humbly kneeled down in front of him so he could see their faces. Look and see. We are your servants. Joseph responded saying, do not fear me. I am not the Almighty. I cannot take the place of the Almighty. But as for you, you thought and desired evil against me. You devised evil against me, but the Almighty had already considered me. The Almighty was mindful of me and He esteemed me. He had already purposed me. The plan was invented and purposed to come to pass by HIM. So, as it is this day, to sustain life for an exceedingly great number of people, to keep them from sickness, to help them grow, to help them restore their health from faintness, and to save their lives from death. You do not need to fear me. I will nourish you and your children. Joseph spoke kindly to his brothers and comforted them. Joseph lived in Egypt, he and his father Jacob's house. Joseph lived one hundred ten years. Joseph was caused to see Ephraim's (**Eff-rhy-eem**) children to their third generation. Joseph considered them. He had experiences with them. He learned about them. Machir (**Mah-hear**), the son of Manasseh (**Mah-nay-sheh**), brought his children to be upon Joseph's knees. In time, Joseph spoke to brothers saying, I am dying. When I am dead, the Almighty will remember you and make a friendly visit to you. He will watch over you and attend to you. He has appointed an overseer and you will be committed into his care. At the Almighty's judgment, the Almighty will punish and hurt the people in the land of Egypt, then He will bring you out of this land onto the land that He promised to our forefather Abraham, to our grandfather Isaac, and to our father Jacob. Pay attention to the overseer and observe him or the Almighty will visit you to judge you and punish you. The sons of Jacob, Joseph's brothers, all his brethren took an oath to Joseph. They spoke saying, we will carry your bones away from here. Joseph was one hundred ten years old when he died. His brethren embalmed him and Joseph was put in a coffin in Egypt.

www.ingramcontent.com/pod-product-compliance
Lightning Source LLC
Chambersburg PA
CBHW020122130526
44591CB00032B/340